EXTERMINATING ISIS

Introduction

In 2016, I was responsible for the deaths of over 600 people. They deserved to die—all of them. They were the bad guys, the evil of our time. History will not grant the Islamic State a redemption arc. I belonged to a strike cell that killed the enemy by the hundreds with aircraft, drones, and artillery. I don't lose sleep over what we did. However, I still struggle with how easy it was. Technology turned warfare into a game, and we treated it as such. Human beings became statistics, their deaths a quantifiable measure of our success. Where historical buildings stood proud, rubble remains. We embraced the darkness, finding humor where others may have found sorrow. Without a threat from the technologically inferior foe in this war of missiles and drones, we thrived. Out of this, we occasionally found we had lost ourselves, and the reality of warfare once again set in. Those moments of the campaign made me reflect on my morality. It made me think about the man I was and how easily we could all change.

What follows is not a tale of adversity or overcoming obstacles. There is no great antagonist to defeat or a hero to root for. It's a tale of slaughter, extermination, and my role in it as the rocket-artillery liaison officer. It's a story of the men and women who were asked to commit a necessary evil day in and day out for months on end, and a sad recounting of how they coped in an environment that let them distance themselves from their choices. It's a glimpse behind the curtain of a technological war and into the hearts of the soldiers who fought it.

CHAPTER I

A Grand Adventure

It wasn't my war. It was supposed to be someone else's problem.

I never dreamed of becoming a soldier; I never had any aspirations of serving my country or going to war. I didn't have some underlying patriotic itch or sense of duty. In fact, the military wasn't something discussed at all in my house when I was growing up. If recruiters sent pamphlets or made phone calls, my mom screened them. America's wars were just something on television. They were problems for other families from some other part of the country. Out of sight, out of mind. The mantra of my youth.

I was still in high school when the United States invaded Iraq and quickly defeated the Iraqi military. I remember watching President George Bush on television standing on an aircraft carrier in front of the "Mission Accomplished" banner. Iraq and Afghanistan were set to be the wars of someone else's generation, a short historical anomaly for the young men and women a few years older than me; a crisis in some foreign land most people my age couldn't find on a map and sadly still can't. If only that were the case. Instead, these wars crossed numerous generations and defined an era. I was one of many who would participate in the Global War on Terror, a crusade against an ideology and a blank check for violence around the world. Parents and their children would fight in the same worthless towns for a cause many still don't fully understand.

The Army wasn't my destiny, or at least that's what I thought, right up until I signed up during a college career fair gone wrong. After working odd jobs for two years in college, I needed to figure out what to do after earning my degree. The youth in America are told a great myth: if you get good grades and go to college, a career will be waiting upon graduation. This is a fairy tale. In reality, most of my friends initially kept the same jobs they had as students, just with more hours and a whole lot of debt. Companies weren't looking for 22-year-olds with almost no work experience. Even government agencies like the Federal Bureau of Investigation wanted applicants who had lived life after college, applicants who had begun a career. There was no obvious answer for those without a clear vision of what they wanted to be when they grew up.

But the Army is always hiring. Because of the wars, the service had ample money to commit to recruiting efforts. This meant the Army could guarantee me a job when I graduated, as well as pay for my last two years of school. I needed no additional incentives. In the summer of 2007, right before starting my junior year at the University of Wahington, I signed up for the Reserve Officers Training Corps. I had found a career. It was more than that, though. The Army ended up being exactly what I needed, filling a void I didn't know existed. Military service has meaning, a purpose beyond just making money. It was different than the jobs I had worked in college. It was something I could be proud of.

We were not selling a product or dealing with customers. Instead, we were preparing for something, a crucible we would face together, the pinnacle event of our lives. We were a team, something I had been sorely missing. I played multiple sports in high school. At best, I was an average athlete, but it was still part of my identity. Like most kids, I had some unrealistic expectations that I would be able to play sports forever. But a lackluster college football tryout and an abysmally short-lived mixed martial arts career ended the professional-athlete delusion.

The Army provided me with a similar feeling, though. I was back on the field, building camaraderie through shared hardships and preparing to take on a rival, albeit in a much more serious game. It just felt right. Most of the training we did while I was still in school was generic Army stuff, the things you often see in the movies: painting faces, marksmanship, camping in the woods, and lots of running. It was fun. I have fond memories of singing songs on cold, overcast mornings in Seattle, running to the famous Fremont Troll, and smelling the fresh, clean breeze off Lake Washington. It was a good, gradual introduction to the Army that included a lot less yelling than I expected.

However, before I graduated, I had the opportunity to intern with an actual Army unit. In the summer of 2008, after completing my culminating cadet training event, I spent a few weeks shadowing some lieutenants at Fort Sill, Oklahoma, the home of the artillery. Beyond simply being exposed to the nuances of day-to-day Army life, which was much less glamorous than I imagined, the unit I was a part of for the summer gave me some first-hand experience with cannon and rocket-artillery systems, hoping to inspire me to join their ranks. This culminated with a live-fire artillery mission.

I nervously walked out to the rocket-artillery launcher, ready to actually do an Army thing, to stop pretending I was a soldier once a week at college. However, I didn't have any of my own equipment except for my uniform. To safely train, I had to scrounge around to borrow what I could. By the time I put together a set, including what I later discovered were extra unnecessary items, I looked absolutely ridiculous. Side note: playing jokes on the new guy is a foundational military game, a lesson I would learn many times in my career.

My helmet bounced around with each step, constantly covering my eyes every few seconds, a problem I quickly learned to remedy by jerking my head back to shift the oversized headgear back into place. My *Desert Storm*-era body armor hung half-open, clearly made for someone much smaller. I looked like Chris Farley doing his "Fat Guy in a Little Coat" routine. To make matters worse, tiny, mismatched knee pads strangled my legs, forcing me to waddle or risk ripping my pants. But I kept moving, determined to get out of the heat and into the vehicle that awaited me.

I knew I was on the receiving end of a joke. Despite their best efforts to hold in their laughs, the snickers of those who sent me on my way filled my ears as I plodded along. A rite of passage, one of many I would eventually navigate. I still didn't feel like a soldier, though, at least not until I got into the cab of the multiple-launch rocket system.

My clothes clung to me like a second layer of skin and sweat poured down my face as if a pipe had burst inside my helmet. We baked in the

Oklahoma sun, cooking in the metal box that was our vehicle. So much for cooling off. Grins crept on the faces of the two soldiers serving as my guides. They enjoyed my suffering a little too much.

I was uncomfortable and looked downright silly. I was out of my element and, by the looks on their faces, they sensed it. I had never really been around real soldiers who operated dangerous and technical machines every day, only cadets like me and a few cadre officers. I hadn't experienced the real Army, whatever that was.

However, after a minute or two, I had a realization. These soldiers were just as uncomfortable around me as I was around them. It wasn't just because I had a weird cadet rank on my chest they probably hadn't seen before, or that I was a potential future boss; I was an outsider. I had entered their domain, thrust upon them against their wishes. They were forced to put on a show.

Eventually, we settled in and got ready to make the mad contraption go boom, a fun pastime of young military men and women around the world.

The soldiers did all the technical work to prepare the launcher to fire; I was just along for the ride, afraid to touch anything I wasn't supposed to. I quickly discovered that live-fire exercises have a rigid script, which meant we didn't have to drive very far or make any decisions. Instead, the soldiers typed firing data into the on-board computer to aim the rocket pod toward the impact area, all in accordance with the script.

"All set, sir, flip this switch when you're ready," one of them finally instructed. They had done this a hundred times; this mission was for me. However, what they didn't include in those basic instructions was to brace for impact.

I flipped the switch, and a massive explosion followed; the launcher blasted a training rocket into the air. I had watched a few missions before getting into the launcher for my turn, so I knew it would be loud. War is inherently loud, even when just practicing. However, I was not prepared for the sheer force that accompanied the explosion. It violently jerked me to the side. My stomach followed a millisecond later before rejoining my body in its usual position and letting me settle back into my seat to try to compose myself. It took a second to regain my senses. The roar of laughter that followed was as loud as the initial explosion, and I noticed the other two in the cab laughing hysterically at my reaction. Clearly, they were used to the ferocity of the firing sequence, and this wasn't the first time they had taken a visitor in their launcher.

Practice rockets are fired directly off the side of the launcher cab. For the crew, it was like getting T-boned at an intersection. It was awesome! I don't know why I liked it so much, but I was hooked. My first fire mission was an adrenaline rush and an unforgettable experience that shaped the type of officer I would become.

After I returned my borrowed gear, I started imagining myself as a rocket-artillery soldier in some foreign country, driving around a battlefield and unleashing destruction. This was my envisioned future, what it would mean for me to be a real soldier. It didn't take long to know I would become the rocket guy.

Shortly after my experience at Fort Sill, I was commissioned onto active duty the summer of 2009 as a second lieutenant field-artillery officer, becoming a member of the US Army's "King of Battle" (so named for the destructive nature of artillery and its historical role as the most casualty producing weapon on the battlefield). I was ready to do my part, to rain death down on the enemies of our nation. I was excited to have a chance to contribute to the wars in Iraq and Afghanistan, to do my duty, and to have those defining experiences that would shape the man I would become.

However, while I would get my opportunity to deploy overseas, the coalition managing the war in Iraq didn't need much artillery this late in the war. The Global War on Terror and my role in it would be nothing like I had imagined as a cadet running around playing Army.

CHAPTER 2

King Without a Crown

Join the Army; travel the world.

I had very little experience firing artillery in my first few years in the Army, most of which was under supervision during my six-month officer introductory course at Fort Sill, Oklahoma in 2010. I tried to convince the Army to assign me to a rocket-artillery unit for my first assignment, but there are only so many of those units and new lieutenants have little input in determining their career path. Instead, I got assigned to a mechanized unit at Fort Riley, Kansas, the home of the historic First Infantry Division, commonly known as the "Big Red One." I spent most of my early military years as a fire-support officer assigned to armor and infantry units, with only a short stint with the artillery.

It didn't matter what type of artillery unit I was assigned to early on, though. My first two deployments were not in a conventional artillery role. In fact, we didn't even bring our weapon systems with us when we deployed. Instead, our cannons stayed in America. The Army was using field-artillery units in Iraq and Afghanistan for all sorts of missions, from guarding bases to patrolling neighborhoods. We deployed as generalists, just random bodies for senior commanders to throw at problems. This often meant a lot of walking and sitting around; a very different kind of war than the one I envisioned.

In preparation for my first deployment with the Big Red One, I had the opportunity to conduct a rotation at the Joint Readiness Training Center (JRTC) in Louisiana. However, conventional combat was the furthest thing from our minds. Instead, we knew the upcoming deployment to Iraq would be a counter-insurgency mission. We focused on how to build relationships, not on fighting an enemy. I even received a multi-week Arabic and Iraqi culture class, which only confirmed what my high school Spanish teacher identified years prior—I'm terrible at learning foreign languages.

For artillerymen specifically, the Army's training focus shifted away from firing cannons and rockets toward conducting intelligence operations at the company level. I took charge of a makeshift company intelligence support team of five soldiers, and the Army provided our team some unique training on battlefield-tracking systems, intelligence-sharing software, and a nifty tool called the biometrics automated toolset system, or BATS, that we used to gather biometric data. With this equipment, the JRTC cadre taught us how to collect fingerprints, iris scans, and facial-recognition data of suspected insurgents.

My unit deployed in late 2010, on Veterans Day weekend, no less. Sadly, there was no free Applebee's for me that year. I had three distinct missions on that deployment, only one of which fit my duty description.

First, I served as a company intelligence planner. This meant conducting route analysis and debriefing soldiers after patrols. This wasn't what I signed up for, but I found it pretty easy, and it forced me to learn a lot about the greater Baghdad area.

Second, I partnered with the Iraqi military at our small compound. This task came with a lot of responsibilities, the most pressing of which was tracking detainees at the small prison on our installation. We collected the biometric data of the prisoners, taking pictures of hundreds of people's eyeballs and uploading them into an extensive database. I have no idea what ever happened to all that data, but I guess most of the people who we took pictures of are probably dead now, so it doesn't matter much. Working with the Iraqi military in this way left a lasting impression on me, a very negative impression.

Finally, I spent much of my time walking the streets of Baghdad, staying close to my commander, and remaining ready to coordinate air support if we were attacked. Luckily, we didn't get attacked. Instead, we just did a lot of walking, a constant reminder to the Iraqi people that we were still there and hadn't abandoned them. Not yet, anyway. While I didn't have the violent engagements with the enemy I expected, I did get some awesome photos of me in downtown Baghdad.

Still, throughout the trip, I never felt like an artilleryman. In fact, I'm not even sure I felt like a soldier. I'm not sure I have ever felt like a soldier. What a weird thing to reflect on, having now served in the Army for over fifteen years.

I don't know what most people who join the military think they are getting themselves into or how wearing the uniform would change them. For me, whatever was supposed to happen didn't. I didn't have that life-changing event that would usher me into adulthood. At the time, I felt like an imposter wearing a costume, a boy still just pretending to play Army.

My first deployment didn't feel like war—an incredibly selfish thought, given that numerous service members in my brigade paid the ultimate sacrifice on the trip. Instead, this mission was scripted to be one of those heartwarming war stories you read about where the young leader learns to appreciate a new culture, befriending the unit interpreter or a local businessman. This was not my experience. I grew to hate the Iraqis. I had no faith in their corrupt military and didn't trust any of their citizens. This was the consequence of an insurgency.

My unit was one of the last in the country, helping officially end the war in 2011. After more than eight years, the US military was finally out of Iraq, at least temporarily. In hindsight, it was cool to be a part of something historic, to conduct the quiet withdrawal of US forces from a significant conflict. However, at the time, I was just glad to leave and didn't care if the country burned in our wake. Fun fact—it pretty much did.

With the Iraq war over and Afghanistan soon to follow, or so we optimistically thought, the military shifted back to focusing on warfighting, abandoning counter-insurgency training. In 2012, I left the armor battalion I had deployed to Iraq with and took over a Paladin platoon—a self-propelled artillery piece that looks more like a tank than a cannon. We began preparing for the next great tank-on-tank war with the Russian hordes, culminating with a trip to the National Training Center (NTC) in Death Valley, California.

We drove around the desert for a few weeks, trying to survive against the resident Army unit stationed at NTC as an opposing force. I quickly discovered that artillery units struggle in this kind of fight. My platoon spent more time moving than shooting, fearing the enemy artillery, and for good reason. While neither side fired any actual artillery rounds in our mock battle, my platoon lost the artillery duel. In fact, I notionally "died" twice to enemy artillery barrages that countered our missions.

The first time I died my whole platoon got destroyed by enemy rockets, solidifying my gut instincts about the future of rocket artillery. The evaluator brought us back to life after the engagement, like a child hitting the reset button in a video game. The second time, it was just me and my driver that got hit. They assessed me as "wounded" and used me as a training tool to evaluate the brigade's medical procedures. My platoon transported me by ground to the medical station where I was triaged and subsequently wrapped in a foil blanket to stay warm while I awaited a surgeon. When the unit chaplain came in to read my last rites, the whole training event got weirdly real. They failed to save me, and I had to wait two days in a holding area until my commander came to pick me up as a "replacement" lieutenant.

While NTC proved to be good training, it was still just training. I wanted more, I didn't just want to practice.

Once we were back in Kansas, I found out one of the other platoon leaders got offered a fire support job with an aviation unit headed to Afghanistan. Why not me? Outraged, I asked our battalion commander if I could compete for the assignment, but that's not how deployments work. However, the division had recently picked up some strange missions across Africa, and he found me something to do. But it wouldn't involve much artillery.

Barely two years after returning home from Iraq, I was back overseas. This type of turnaround was the norm for many of us during this time, and for some it was even quicker, especially earlier in the wars. My second deployment, while a more enjoyable situation than the first, still didn't provide me with the warfare experience I thought I needed.

I deployed to the Horn of Africa in December 2013 for a seven-month assignment. I spent most of my time in the small country of Djibouti (pronounced "Joe-Booty" ... not really, but it makes me smile to say it that way). My time in Africa was a unique and incredible opportunity. Still, it, too, differed drastically from what I had signed up to do as an artilleryman. I had just been promoted to captain and was put in charge of the fire-support section of an infantry battalion. Our mission was to conduct theater security cooperation, which meant partnering with neighboring countries on the continent and building military relationships to help strengthen the region, primarily through training and exercises.

Like my first deployment, we didn't take any of our artillery equipment with us. So much for being a part of the "King of Battle," more like a king without a crown. But we weren't there to fight a war.

Our primary task was to act as a quick-reaction force, able to reinforce several different embassies in East Africa and, if needed, help evacuate non-combatants. This was a fairly new mission, and it seemed to me to be a Defense Department response to the 2012 Benghazi incident where the US ambassador was killed.

Just days after arriving in the Horn of Africa, the South Sudanese Civil War broke out, and we got busy. A significant portion of my unit went to Juba, South Sudan, to help evacuate American citizens and strengthen the US Embassy's defenses. I stayed in Djibouti as a liaison officer to the Horn of Africa headquarters.

I watched the civil war happen on drone feeds while I sat in an office roughly a thousand miles away. I was surprised at how far our technology had advanced. It was incredible to have that tactical awareness, watching battles unfold with the combatants unaware they were being observed. Warfare had evolved for the technologically superior force, like the United States. The people in the air-conditioned office had grown in importance, becoming the puppet masters of tactical actions without assuming any of the inherent risks.

However, at the same time, there was a sense of helplessness. Even though we had the capabilities, we couldn't act even if we wanted to. This was not our war; we were simply spectators. I would get this chance again a few years later, and with those drone feeds we would act, exterminating a technologically inferior foe.

I did have one chance to be an artilleryman in Africa. I was selected to evaluate and train an Ethiopian Army artillery unit preparing for combat. Because the opinions of a captain wouldn't carry much weight with the Ethiopians, I spent a few weeks pretending to be Colonel Brennan, wearing civilian clothes and sporting the only beard I've ever grown in my life. While it was not a great beard, I sure felt cool trying to grow it. Maybe I'll grow one when I retire and become a stereotypical military veteran.

This training opportunity was great. It was the closest I had felt to combat, albeit in someone else's war. The Ethiopian unit I worked with was gearing up for combat operations in Somalia and quickly found themselves in action after our time together. They took their old Soviet D-30 cannons to war in a conflict that most of the Western world remains oblivious to. They were artillerymen doing their job in the war of their time; I was envious.

What a strange feeling.

I would eventually get my chance. While I conducted operations in Africa, a new foe rose to power, a worldwide threat that couldn't be ignored. Our problems in the Middle East weren't over. I don't know if they will ever be.

CHAPTER 3

ISIS

I hate them. I hate them for what they did, what they represent, and for what they made us do.

I sat on the edge of my seat in horror, shocked and discouraged to see the Middle East descend back into chaos. I watched the news intently as the war unfolded before our eyes, the voices of the reporters occasionally drowned out by distant explosions. The camera zoomed in on a black flag being raised, the wind snapping it into view. It was the symbol of the growing threat, the flag of an extremist organization that was spreading like a virus, unstoppable. Another city had fallen. Iraq was no longer a problem of our past. With each city that fell, each mile of territory captured, it became more apparent it was a problem the United States couldn't ignore for much longer.

I had said my goodbyes to that awful place in 2011, never expecting to return. We left Iraq to stand on its own, albeit with a massive military trained and equipped by the United States. I certainly didn't think I would be heading back to Iraq; we had won that war. Well, we had ended that war.

But the Middle East was no better off after the United States withdrew its military than when it invaded eight years beforehand. In fact, the region we left behind in 2011 was in a shambles. Numerous countries in North Africa and the Middle East were undergoing transformation, some for the better, some into chaos. The Arab Spring—a sequence of uprisings and violent protests—was reshaping the region. While the Arab Spring initially appeared to be a movement toward freedom and democracy, it was underwritten with violence and met with stark resistance by those who could cling to their power.

As American operations ceased in Iraq, it was still unclear how the region would shape out, and the secondary effects of the Arab Spring couldn't have been predicted. Numerous countries deposed their leaders, demanding change and a voice in their future government. Some leaders met protests head on, cracking down violently on those who took to the streets. This action plunged nations like Libya and Syria into civil war.

Among this chaos, the evil of our generation rose to prominence. In late 2011, Al Qaeda in Iraq, a terrorist organization that had plagued the US military for a decade, took advantage of the power vacuum created by the American withdrawal and the collapse of local governments. It extended its operations into Syria, sowing chaos and strengthening the insurgency there. By the summer of 2012, the organization had grown substantially and refocused its efforts in Iraq, capitalizing on the US absence. But the attacks weren't very effective.

Arguably, it was simply a renewal of a terror campaign, something Iraq was already quite familiar with. However, everything changed in the spring of 2013 with the fall of the Syrian city of Raqqa. The insurgent groups in the two nations shared common interests and joined in their cause.

It was a rebranding, and the combined strength of these organizations created a new, highly dangerous threat to the region, establishing themselves as the Islamic State of Iraq and Syria. ISIS. The name, pronounced as a word, transcended the acronym, and captured the world's attention.

The rapid growth of ISIS was remarkable, and the world took notice as its horrific actions dominated media outlets. The extremist organization stood apart from the terrorists who had harassed the American military for the previous decade, the ones that had threatened my teammates and me in 2011. What made ISIS different was not the shock-and-awe inherent to a terror campaign. These types of activities have been happening around the world, and been conducted by all types of groups, for years. Instead, they captured territory, fielding an army like a nation state. With Raqqa as its capital, ISIS began securing territory in the failed state of Syria. By the end of 2013, this conquest extended into the heart of Iraq.

ISIS fanned the flames of revolt inside Iraq, helping other Sunni insurgents destabilize the region. Just as it did in Syria, ISIS began securing territory in Iraq. On a larger scale, this meant extending its capital from Raqqa, primarily capturing and controlling the border between the two nations. These territorial gains allowed ISIS to move freely from its bases in Syria to deep into Iraq along two conquest paths.

One direction led north towards Mosul. On paper, Mosul was a formidable stronghold for the Iraqi military. However, the Iraqis defending the city crumbled in the face of an attack. The Iraqi security forces and federal police numbered tens of thousands each. ISIS, on the other hand, had barely 1,500 fighters. Although they were estimated to be outnumbered fifteen to one, ISIS achieved a fast and decisive victory.

In June 2014, Mosul was taken after less than a week of fighting. The Iraqi military defending the city fell apart, and thousands were killed or wounded. Those captured were executed, with estimates in the thousands. ISIS raised its black flags in Mosul, as they would in many places across the country.

ISIS excelled at information operations and propaganda, and the infamous black flag became a symbol impossible to ignore. Hundreds of thousands of civilians fled Mosul, accompanied by thousands of Iraqi military deserters. ISIS grew stronger, pillaging the town for supplies, securing abandoned military equipment, and swelling its ranks with liberated terrorists from local prisons. The extremist organization consolidated its gains in the north and remained immovable for the next few years.

The second line of effort for the ISIS advance led directly to Baghdad, Iraq's capital. While the capital never fell, surrounding cities like Fallujah and Ramadi were not so lucky. Both fell quickly in January 2014, but Iraqi security forces continued to fight. Ramadi was back in Iraqi control by mid-March. However, Fallujah was lost, black flags blowing in the wind. The Iraqi military was unprepared for the fight against ISIS, and it didn't take long for the organization to raise the flag over countless other cities, highlighting its successful conquest.

With each victory, ISIS grew stronger by recruiting locals, freeing prisoners, and scavenging equipment. At the same time, the Iraqi military became weaker. The loss of crucial terrain, critical equipment, and thousands of troops as casualties and deserters complicated the already dire circumstances, not to mention that this new foe seemed unstoppable, securing a psychological advantage over the Iraqi military with every successive victory.

There was no denying the severity of the situation; Iraq would soon collapse into a failed state. To make matters worse, ISIS showed the world its brutality, filming executions and posting beheading videos online. The terrorist organization was a plague, and it had to be addressed.

The United States responded. However, because the US political appetite to reinvade the country or put "boots on the ground" was nonexistent, the initial response was minimal. So, instead of an invasion, the United States increased its financial support to the Iraqi Government and sent some special-operations advisors to help the Iraqi military. But anyone who had worked with the Iraqis before knew this wouldn't be enough. The Iraqi military wasn't fighting back, and the United States could not simply buy them courage.

As I watched the events unfold, I couldn't help but think that the American military involvement in the conflict would soon grow. The biggest indicator for those of us paying attention was when the military decided to establish a forward operations center near the US Embassy in Baghdad. In my eyes, we were on the slippery slope back to war, only this time nobody seemed to care. I quickly found myself at a crossroads and was surprised by my desire to take the path less travelled, the path that led me back to Iraq.

CHAPTER 4

All Roads Lead Back

Initially, I didn't care about the Arab Spring, nations in the Middle East and North Africa collapsing, or even the rise of ISIS. I certainly didn't think I would be heading back to Iraq; we had won that war.

After returning home from Africa in the summer of 2014, I had the opportunity to attend my captain-level professional military education with the United States Marine Corps in Quantico, Virginia. Over the next 10 months, the ISIS problem slowly crept into our conversations. Iraq had been a defining moment for many officers at varying times in their careers, from the 2003 invasion to the 2007 surge, and even the 2011 withdrawal. The Iraq War, as ugly as it had been, was over. An American return to Iraq raised questions about the military's sacrifices in the decade-long conflict, diminishing the work of those who had risked everything.

At the same time, the US military had just gone through drastic cuts. Army captains and majors across the force had received the dreaded "pink slip," ending their military careers abruptly. We were facing a drawdown, the inherent price of the peace dividend. Sadly, in the profession of arms, war is good for business. A conflict increases promotion rates, military pay, and the populace's perception of the military. In turn, feelings concerning our potential return to Iraq were mixed for many. Shortly into the course, the conflict abroad escalated further; many of us had to make hard decisions about what we would do after we graduated.

In August 2014, after realizing the financial support and advisor strategy was doomed to fail, the United States formed a coalition and began an air campaign to enable the success of the Iraqi military by weakening the enemy through strike warfare. While immediate crises needed to be addressed, the underlying goal was to stop the spread of ISIS and contain it. It didn't take long for decision makers to recognize there wouldn't be a quick fix to the problem. The airstrikes alone couldn't defeat the extremist organization. Airpower is a great tool, but unless the objective was the destruction of Iraq (which it felt like it was at times), bombing only provided a partial solution. Tactically, this type of campaign is designed to augment land forces. The coalition needed someone to root out the enemy from areas we couldn't identify from the sky, secure critical supply routes, and control terrain after the enemy was defeated.

Sadly, this meant the coalition would have to rely on the Iraqi military to mount counteroffensives, a force few of us had any faith in. There was also a plan to recruit willing Syrians to help with this cause, but these efforts produced few additional fighters. Instead, the United States decided to fully support the Iraqis with everything except ground forces. This meant intelligence, logistics, and strike capabilities. In October 2014, to formalize the new strategy, the Pentagon designated the mission against ISIS as Operation *Inherent Resolve*. Like it or not, we were once again committed to fixing Iraq.

It was initially unclear what this meant for me and the other officers waiting to find out our next assignments. Overall, it looked like the United States would gradually return to Iraq in earnest. Hell, I assumed combat forces were likely to be committed shortly after the air campaign faltered, which it was bound to do. At a minimum, if airpower was how the United States would fight the war, there might be a role for long-range artillery.

Selfishly, I was excited. As much as I had no desire to return to that wasteland, this new conflict could be my only chance to do my job, something I had not done in my previous two deployments: fire artillery at the enemy.

I made up my mind halfway through my training with the Marines. If the opportunity arose, I would get myself back into the fight. It's weird to say aloud in reflection, but I wanted to have a real Army experience, whatever the hell that is. I needed to feel like I did my part, like I contributed to something great and historic. At the same time, I wanted to have cool stories to tell my kids and grandkids. While I may have had a couple of deployments under my belt already, I had missed the fighting and, to be honest, felt pretty self-conscious about it.

There is a famous quote from Douglas MacArthur: "The soldier above all prays for peace, for it's the soldier who must suffer and bear the deepest wounds and scars of war." While true, there is another side to that coin—every generation has young men searching for opportunities to prove themselves, make their mark on history, and be part of something great. The glamorization of combat and glory leads many young soldiers and leaders to crave the conflict, to test themselves, and to discover the type of person they are. Out of this ignorance, selfishness, and lack of empathy for those who must inherently suffer in war, I saw the turmoil in Iraq as the next great adventure, a chance to gain unique experiences and build my credibility as a combat-arms officer.

I began watching events unfold in Iraq much more closely after deciding I wanted to get back into the fight. The crisis continued to escalate even after the US commitment. In fact, the ISIS onslaught didn't stop; the extremist organization continued capturing territory, leaving destruction, death, and black flags in its wake. ISIS expanded its control in central Iraq. The town of Kubaysah fell in early October 2014. A few weeks later, the Iraqi military abandoned the Hit region, which lies just northwest of Ramadi on the Euphrates River. ISIS secured more military equipment, and the Iraqi military retreated along with thousands of displaced citizens.

Another conquest, another black flag.

ISIS turned its attention back towards Ramadi, the Al Anbar provincial capital and an operationally significant piece of terrain. The Iraqi military conducted a sustained fight for the first time since ISIS began its advance into the country. Sadly, they eventually quit, conceding the town, and abandoning the citizens trapped inside to a numerically inferior and poorly equipped foe.

This was a significant setback for the coalition, undermining any previous success. To lose resoundingly and flee, even with the support of coalition airpower, sent a powerful message. It was an embarrassment.

It was also a critical lesson for senior leaders, a lesson many who worked directly with the Iraqis already understood. No matter how well trained or equipped, the Iraqi military didn't have the will to fight. There was no solution to this underlying problem, and it undoubtedly factored into the nation's collapse.

Coalition strikes continued over the rest of the year with intermittent success, and Defense Department plans to train ground forces in the region faltered and underproduced. Iraq was a disaster and the strategy to halt ISIS was failing. The war would drag on, and I knew it. I was going to get myself into this fight. When the human resources officer asked me where I wanted to go next, the answer was simple: I wanted to join a rocket-artillery unit, and I wanted to go back to Iraq.

CHAPTER 5

HIMARS

*This was my chance; I wouldn't be left behind even
if I had to write the damn order myself.*

I graduated from the Marine Corps Expeditionary Warfare School in the summer of 2015 as a junior captain. For the first time in my career, the Army gave me some freedom in determining my future, so I finally secured the job in a rocket-artillery unit I had been trying to get since commissioning six years prior. My peers thought I was crazy. I was told it was career suicide to leave the real artillery, the cannons that supported maneuver forces, for a niche rocket capability. Rocket artillery resides at more senior headquarters, supporting divisions, corps, and theater-level operations. There was this perception, and probably still is, that serving in one of these units meant you were no longer around the actual warfighters.

However, I knew the next part of the conflict against ISIS would be fought with precision, more like an air campaign than a land war. US Army infantry battalions wouldn't be in the lead, nor would the cannons that supported them. Rockets were my way to secure a ride overseas and get me a seat at the table. Rocket artillery was going to be my chance to finally engage the enemy.

The Army gave me what I wanted, and in the summer of 2015, I joined the 17th Field Artillery Brigade, the "Thunderbolts," at Fort Lewis, Washington. Unlike my previous unit at Fort Riley that emphasized tanks and infantry fighting vehicles, field artillery was the main show in the Thunderbolt Brigade, with the unit built around two High Mobility Artillery Rocket System battalions (HIMARS, read it as a word, not an acronym). HIMARS launchers are simply trucks with a large rocket pod on top that carries either six rockets or one large missile. Each rocket can be fired individually or as part of a group at targets up to roughly seventy-five kilometers away, and they are incredibly accurate: we could put a rocket through someone's chimney or into the windshield of a parked car.

While the term "rocket" probably primes most people to envision large explosions, these precision weapons were specifically designed to reduce collateral damage and had a surprisingly minimal blast. This feature is critical for operating in an urban environment. There is value in being able to destroy a city block with a couple of bombs. There is also value in being able to precisely destroy a small section of the building a target is hiding in. This is especially true in a city, where the goal is often to defeat threats while damaging the least amount of infrastructure.

Additionally, the systems are light enough to be transported in the back of a cargo aircraft. This meant that if HIMARS were to support the mission against ISIS, the coalition could insert the launchers, personnel, and ammunition across the country without conducting cross-country convoys. This would not only reduce the chances of receiving casualties from an attack while driving from Point A to Point B, but would also allow the coalition to insert them discreetly, avoiding unwanted attention in the war zone and back home.

HIMARS provided a tool to augment the aircraft that had dominated the conflict thus far. The coalition agreed.

In the fall of 2015, the unit I was in received orders to support Operation *Inherent Resolve* starting in January 2016. But the mission only required a single firing battery, plus some minor staff support. This totaled about one hundred twenty-five people at most, and none of the requirements called for the random new captain who had just arrived at the unit.

I needed to get on the list, or I would miss what was likely my last opportunity.

When we first received the orders, it was unclear what our level of involvement would be in the war. Initially, the orders only had the unit going to Kuwait, which is not a fun mission. There was a decent chance the unit would simply be some sort of reserve element, all the soldiers waiting in the desert of Kuwait, ready to advance into Iraq if the situation changed. Still, rumors started circulating that more military capabilities were being pushed north into Iraq to support operations against ISIS. The war was escalating, and my assumptions about the Army gradually building up its footprint had been validated. We eventually received updated mission information from the unit we were slotted to replace. HIMARS had entered the war.

The updated mission requirements had our unit deploying to three different locations. Most of the soldiers would remain at Camp Buehring, Kuwait, the Army's strategic staging base for operations in the Middle East. I had spent a little bit of time there previously. I don't envy anyone who has to do one of these rotations, sharing massive tents, using shower trailers, and having to walk to a porta-potty in the middle of the night to pee. Porta-potties that, at times, had internal temperatures over one-hundred degrees Fahrenheit and were infrequently cleaned, a combination that produces quite an aroma. No, thank you. Our battalion executive officer, a major, would lead this element and be the senior member of the deployment package. The soldiers in Kuwait would continue honing their craft and building partnerships with the Kuwaiti military while they awaited their opportunity to go north into Iraq. Most would have the chance. We did our best to make sure everyone got some of the action; I wasn't the only one who wanted to do what we had trained for.

A small portion of the unit would occupy a newly established rocket-artillery firing point at Al Asad Air Base, Iraq. This once massive military installation had become a shadow of its former self. The base sits about eighty kilometers northeast of Ramadi, just outside the Hit District in Iraq. The group consisted of two launchers, a fire-direction center to calculate mission data, and roughly half a platoon of soldiers led by a lieutenant and a sergeant first class.

I was the perfect candidate for the third spot, at least in my eyes. While missions were fired from Al Asad, the headquarters that coordinated and prosecuted the missions resided in Baghdad at the forward operating center near the embassy. We needed someone to serve as our unit representative, to get HIMARS into the fight. I argued loudly and publicly that I was the best fit for the position. My battalion commander, who planned on remaining in the United States for the duration of the deployment, eventually gave his approval. I'm not sure if it was because I made a convincing argument or if he was just happy to get rid of me. I was not his favorite officer by any means. In fact, we would only talk once or twice while I was away ... and it was never for anything positive.

Our training priorities quickly shifted, and we began preparing for war. However, we would find out, shortly after arriving overseas, that we had trained for the wrong war. We had trained for the type of war we were comfortable with, the kind we had a script for, and had envisioned in our exercises. Because of this, we were not prepared to do our job when we got down range. It's funny, we were able to watch the war unfold so our training requirements shouldn't have been a surprise. I would later find out it's very hard to go off script when conducting training.

The coalition started to make progress against ISIS shortly before we deployed to Iraq. The first significant victory occurred in December 2015 when the Iraqi military, backed by Western air power, liberated Ramadi. I use "liberated" loosely. While ISIS was indeed expelled from the area, the cost of doing so was high. The city had been systematically destroyed, one building and one precision munition at a time. The Iraqi military had begun the operation in October 2015 by first isolating the town to prevent ISIS reinforcements. Once complete, house-to-house fighting began as Iraqi forces captured neighborhoods one at a time in their march to the city center. It was slow, methodical, and bloody.

Each city block presented a new obstacle, slowing the advance and risking the operation falling apart—another setback the coalition couldn't afford. So, buildings were destroyed. Thousands of buildings. Additionally, the coalition cratered roads, downed bridges, and damaged critical infrastructure beyond repair. The city would never be the same; it was rubble. This fight highlighted the inherent challenges of urban warfare, challenges that would continue in this war, regardless of how well we avoided unnecessary collateral damage.

With the success at Ramadi, the coalition had achieved its first significant victory and stopped the spread of ISIS. Still, the terrorist organization controlled numerous cities in the Al Anbar province, including Fallujah, Hit, and Kubaysah. With renewed confidence in the Iraqi military's willingness to fight, the coalition shifted gears and began preparing to conduct a massive offensive to defeat ISIS, one city at a time. The battle for central Iraq would be fought and decided in 2016. It was at this point in the operation that I joined the fight.

CHAPTER 6

Home Sweet Home

It's a shithole! It's dirty, it stinks, and the people are just not nice. One out of five stars, I don't recommend it.

As I stepped off the plane and into the scorching hot embrace of the desert, I found myself questioning some of my life decisions. What was I doing here? Standing in the sun produced a painful experience drastically different from the balmy weather of Washington State, where I was stationed. Every breath burned my nostrils and sapped my energy as my body fought to adjust. Even though I had lived in Iraq a few years prior, I was unprepared for the initial shock. I couldn't believe how hot it was in February. How do people become accustomed to this type of weather? The desert life is not for me.

The smell was worse than the heat. I had forgotten how dirty Iraq was, with garbage literally strewn everywhere outside our little gated communities. While the heat felt foreign, the distinct smell was not. Powerful scents are one of the strongest links to memories and emotions. In this case, the subtle aroma of dirty porta-potties and hot garbage cooking in the sun triggered a flood of memories from my first deployment in 2010.

It felt strange to be back. I never thought I would see the desert wasteland again after we left the Iraqis to their own devices five years prior. The area was eerily similar to my first trip, yet somehow an incredibly foreign experience. I had lived near the airport for a couple of months in 2011 as my unit prepared to redeploy home, but it was different then. When I left as a young lieutenant, the airport was surrounded by the massive Victory Base Complex, an installation rivaling any military compound in the United States; it had housed and sustained over forty thousand service members and was the heart of coalition operations in the country for years. When I arrived in 2016, the base was worn down and abandoned, a ghost town. It was a shell of its former self, serving only as a logistics hub and supporting transient folks like me.

The roads in Iraq were closed to the US military. There would be no convoys or patrolling this time around. However, only two of us needed to move forward to the headquarters near the embassy to work in the strike cell. For me and my noncommissioned officer, finding a helicopter and hitching a ride to the international zone—one of the last remnants of the US occupation—was not hard. I had done a similar route a dozen times on the ground when I was previously deployed. I knew the terrain. I had driven the infamous Route Irish that connected the bases and walked the neighborhoods in the area in 2011. But the country looked so much different from the air; peaceful even. The most dangerous aspect of my first deployment had been nullified as I no longer had to worry about roadside improvised explosive devices. That said, helicopter rides always make me kind of nervous; as flying machines, they just don't seem like they should be able to stay airborne.

We arrived at our final destination in Baghdad in the middle of the night and found some transient tents to bunk down in until we got settled. The compound, Union III, was tiny; it was maybe a quarter to a half mile around, with a single road wrapping around the base. There was plenty of housing available, and I eventually moved into a repurposed shipping container that provided all the comforts of home. Not really, but it was pretty nice for a combat zone. I shared a single room with one other captain, and we had access to a bathroom for the two of us to share. More importantly, it had a powerful air conditioner that let us escape the harsh conditions outside. Overall, it was a dramatically better setup than I would have had back in Kuwait.

Although the base was small, it had some of the best amenities a soldier could ask for. The gym was in the compound's center, directly between the housing area and my workstation. It was a massive facility with a wide assortment of fitness equipment. Some people, including me, hosted fitness classes to break up the monotony of the trip. The dining facility was directly across the street from the gym. It was always well stocked, and no limits were ever placed on how much one could eat—our own personal buffet. I always got my money's worth. That's a joke; it was free, so I guess I got my tax dollars' worth.

It was easy to forget where we were, to appreciate the living conditions and just relax. But then I would walk by one of the security gates guarded by the Iraqi military and that feeling would quickly disappear. I didn't trust them. I was always on edge when I thought about them protecting us. I knew they wouldn't risk their lives for us. Hell, they had shown an unwillingness to risk their lives for their country or their comrades, why do it for the infidels? The idea that my life was ever in their hands made me uncomfortable, and I often felt anxious, hyperalert, and ready to defend myself whenever they were around. It was a constant reminder we were not there for a vacation, no matter how well we were taken care of.

Besides the random security checkpoints on the base, I didn't have to see Iraqis often or have to work directly with their military on this deployment. This was good, as I wouldn't have been the best candidate to help build relationships. They were not my friends, nor did I think in the slightest that they were our allies.

While my mission might have been to support them, Iraqis weren't allowed in the strike cell where I worked. In fact, only Five Eyes nations—the United States, Australia, Canada, New Zealand, and the United Kingdom—were allowed access. Instead, a senior US military officer often served as a sort of go-between when information needed to be relayed to Iraqi military leaders, or if they needed to relay something to us. He was a combat version of *Seinfeld*'s Kramer, regularly sliding through our door unannounced and highly strung.

An Army division headquarters manned the installation and oversaw all operations in the country. When I arrived at Union III, the headquarters was in the middle of a transition. The 82nd Airborne Division, which had managed the Ramadi campaign, finished its mission in March 2016, and the 101st Airborne Division took over mission responsibility for Iraq. This transition between the units didn't really impact me because I had deployed as an individual. It didn't matter who my bosses were, although the ambiguity of who I answered to would bite me in the ass midway through the deployment, nearly ending my career.

At the end of the day, what unit called the shots wasn't important. The transition did let me stop being the new guy, though. It was nice to no longer be the outsider who hadn't been there for all the hard work that went into liberating Ramadi.

The coalition higher headquarters, an Army corps commanded by a three-star general, was responsible for the overarching Middle East mission, serving as the theater-level headquarters. Senior leaders at this level set priorities, established rules of engagement, and allocated critical resources like aircraft for all aspects of the mission. This required balancing the responsibility to build partnerships in the region with allies like Jordan and the United Arab Emirates against the inherently resource-taxing combat operations in Iraq and Syria.

While our mission was simply a component of a broader Middle East strategy, we were undoubtedly the main attraction, at least for a few months. There was a short lull in operations during the first few weeks of 2016. However, the Iraqi military was preparing to launch its next major campaign against ISIS by the time I arrived. It wouldn't take long to get into the fight, and central Iraq would demand a theater-wide effort to bring the necessary resources to bear against our foe.

Union III had an operations center to oversee, help plan, and support Iraqi Security Forces in their upcoming endeavor. It was here that a two-star general, the division commander, held daily briefs and received critical updates. The massive building was filled with dozens of officers from various countries and specialties, an auditorium always packed with senior leaders. This was a place a young captain does his best to avoid, a place I entered two to three times in total during the deployment. But senior leaders had a way of finding me. As one of only two HIMARS subject-matter experts (a term I use loosely) on the compound, my opinion carried weight. I needed to be the expert they assumed I was. This meant hitting the books and rehearsing our fire-mission procedures before lives were on the line. When I finally reported to the strike cell, a major I had never met told me I had about forty-eight hours to "get my shit together" before the war would begin again.

CHAPTER 7

Tactics, Techniques, and Procedures

The answers aren't in the book. Sometimes you have to just figure it the fuck out.

The strike cell was not a good place to study, but it was my only option. I couldn't run practice operations anywhere else. The distractions were normally pretty fun, though, especially when I was still the new guy.

"We've got movement!" I heard someone shout from across the room. "Not sure what he's loading in the car, but that's definitely a weapon on his back."

I poked my head up from my little corner to see what was going on. I hadn't figured out what everyone's purpose was, but I still listened intently. I knew my rockets weren't in the fight yet; I had a few more days to prepare. Still, it was hard to focus when a mission was happening. There was something about it. The screens drew everyone in. I stopped running my rehearsals for a few minutes to watch the carnage.

"Shit! He's taking off," the captain continued. "I don't know where he's going, but he sure is in a hurry. We need to take the shot before he clears the target area. The drone has an angle and a clear line of sight. Standing by for final approval."

While I had spent my first few hours in the strike cell trying to figure out how to do my job, the rest of the team was hunting. There weren't many strikes during this period because the Iraqi military was transitioning between campaigns. The area they were observing was pretty much a ghost town at this point, but options were limited until more areas were vetted by the leadership. For now, this meant they weren't letting an easy target slip through their fingers.

It was weird watching the mission unfold. I don't know if the guy even knew he was being followed by the drone. He sure as hell wasn't going to outrun it. I laughed a little as it happened. The last time I was in this situation was when I was in Africa. During that crisis, we all had to just watch, helpless. It wasn't our war. Not this time, though. We weren't just going to play a part in the Iraqi campaigns, we were going to be the judge, jury, and executioner in this technological fight. I didn't know much about the war, but it was clear this was going to be a one-sided conflict, and I was glad to be on the side with the better technology.

Everything happened so fast after the mission got approved. We watched the little box on the screen follow the car as the laser-guided missile headed to its destination. And then it was obliterated. The smoke cleared shortly after. One vehicle destroyed; one enemy killed. Easy mission.

I had seen videos of strikes before. You can find them on the internet if you want a little taste of the action from the safety of your home. But it was different being there when it happened, not knowing exactly how it was going to go. There was some quick celebration after the car exploded, a pat on the back of the drone liaison, and then back to hunting. The strike cell moved on as if it never happened, and I got back on my fancy artillery computer to keep training.

However, two contrasting feelings hit me before I went back to rehearsing my HIMARS missions. First and foremost, I was jealous. What a strange feeling at an inappropriate time. But I wanted my turn. I wanted everyone to cheer me on. I craved the glory and recognition that came with the mission.

At the same time, I was terrified. The reality of the mission set in. I wasn't concerned about killing the enemy or how that would make me feel. The moral question was not a factor at all. In fact, the opposite: I was excited about it. This was precisely what I wanted. It was why I had volunteered for the mission, to do my job instead of just training for it. I wanted them dead. ISIS was evil and needed to be eradicated from the world. I was determined to do my part, my duty. Still, that came with a lot of expectations; I would operate in an environment where failure had severe consequences.

I became acutely aware I wasn't deployed as part of a group of experts advising senior leaders on the employment of rockets. I didn't join a pre-existing team. It was just me, and a lot of people had questions and comments about how we would use HIMARS during the upcoming Iraqi campaign, especially the new team members from the incoming division. My noncommissioned officer partner was brilliant and a necessary addition; he was a technical expert, ensuring everything was done correctly on our fancy field-artillery computer. However, this didn't help sell our capability to everyone else on Union III; nobody cared much about how it worked. They wanted plain language and simple explanations. So, I was on my own when senior officers needed to be briefed on HIMARS capabilities. Everyone would look to me for the ground truth on what rocket artillery could accomplish. I'm a pretty good bullshitter, but that can only go so far.

It's a strange dynamic, being an individual that shows up to support an already established and cohesive team. I didn't participate in any sort of training with the division managing the fight. My noncommissioned officer and I were outsiders to the organization, an unknown element with a distinct patch that stood out in the crowd of uniformed personnel. While we were unknown, there was still an inherent expectation of expertise, an institutional trust the Army had sent the very best to coordinate HIMARS. However, we knew this assumption could quickly be proven wrong when the first rockets started firing, or worse, if they failed to.

I felt like an imposter, concerned someone would somehow expose my lack of knowledge. I spent the early parts of my career in an armored-brigade combat team; my only experience with artillery was planning for the employment of cannons—a dramatically different process from precision rockets. But I had read everything I could, asked the hard questions to the senior rocket-artillery noncommissioned officers in my unit, and even had a couple of practice attempts at being the HIMARS liaison officer during a division command-post exercise and a brigade combat training center rotation.

Still, I didn't feel ready to execute the mission and actually fire rockets at targets in Iraq with the Iraqi military depending on me to eliminate a threat.

I don't think this was from a lack of preparation as much as just insecurity, some underlying idea that, no matter the topic, I'm supposed to know more than I do, that I could never answer "I don't know." I would like to think this is a common feeling in the military. Many likely feel the military culture forces them to display some kind of confident facade, not allowing them to show the slightest hint of weakness for fear someone may pounce on it.

It's hard to tell if this is the case. In my experience, few officers are candid about their doubts, known weaknesses, or previous failures. I wonder if they, too, are insecure, afraid someone might expose their inabilities and chastise them for being anything less than perfect. After serving in the military for over fifteen years, I'm more comfortable following a competent leader with doubts, someone who is open to being challenged appropriately and willing to change, than an overconfident one lacking the humility to acknowledge faults or accept criticism. Sadly, there are plenty of the latter throughout the military.

My unit had spent months training for this mission. Well, kind of. We had trained for something. This was my third deployment; we seemed to train for the wrong war each time. We conducted numerous simulations and field exercises, even battling a made-up notional enemy in a large conventional-military fight. This training culminated with me taking another trip to NTC where we drove around Death Valley overdressed in chemical gear and simulated firing our rockets at a bunch of tanks. To make matters worse, we constantly got our ass kicked by the imaginary enemy rocket-artillery units. A bit of déjà vu from my previous trip and a reminder to never be on the receiving end artillery in real life. As always, it was a great experience and I learned a lot; we all did. But it didn't prepare us for the unique requirements of strike warfare. The training was drastically different to what we knew we would face, different from the reality of the conflict at hand.

It wasn't a secret our mission would revolve more around fire-mission processing and the nuances of technical systems than simply saturating the battlefield with anti-tank munitions. The popular argument is that it's easy to scale down if you are trained for the big fight, the large-scale clash of armies. While that claim may have validity, the tasks were too different in this case, and we had to both unlearn and relearn basic fire-mission procedures. I felt embarrassed by our initial lack of preparedness for the mission at hand.

One of the things that makes rocket artillery so effective for this type of conflict is something called the multiple-precision-aimpoint mission. Because each HIMARS launcher holds six individually programmable rockets, each rocket can be given a different coordinate to hit. For example, when striking a building with three rockets, we can program each rocket to impact a separate structurally important area, increasing the likelihood of an inward collapse versus relying on a big explosion to blow the building apart. Additionally, if we fired those rockets from multiple launchers—let's say five rockets split between two launchers—we could have multiple rockets arrive at nearly the same time.

This was a task we should have become experts on before the deployment. This type of mission was what we needed to practice the most as it was how we would fire almost every rocket-artillery mission in Iraq. Sadly, we had nearly zero experience employing rockets this way when we arrived. We had to learn, and we had to do it quickly. The challenge, however, was creating this mission in the fancy artillery computer system, something we didn't practice beforehand and had to experiment with once in Iraq.

Figuring out how to work through all the little challenges of mission processing consumed most of our time when we first arrived. Still, we identified the necessary workaround to any system issues and established some standard operating procedures. Luckily, we were able to take advantage of a couple of slow days and cram an enormous amount of training and rehearsing into our first 48 hours in Iraq. This included figuring out how and when I would communicate critical information and commands down to the firing point at Al Asad as well as internally to the strike-cell team for airspace clearance, launcher readiness, and actual firing commands.

We eventually captured these training lessons, sharing them with the rest of the unit residing in Kuwait to ensure they were prepared for the unique mission circumstances when they rotated up into Iraq for their turn. Additionally, with the support of soldiers at the HIMARS firing point, I wrote a short article to share with the rest of the artillery community that challenged our standard approach to qualifying our sections on HIMARS before deployments.

Sadly, I happened to work for one of those overconfident leaders who couldn't accept fault and wouldn't acknowledge that his unit was not appropriately trained for its mission. My battalion commander, who didn't deploy with us and experience our fire-mission processing challenges, quashed my article. He told me it was not "in line" with where the artillery community was going. When I argued that was the whole point, to identify issues Army leaders were unaware of, he provided me with a very firm cease and desist, implying he would ruin my career if I disobeyed. I followed these instructions while the threat remained valid, but I didn't give up on the idea.

This was my first time being censored by a senior officer who felt the need to silence my ideas. It wasn't my last. In fact, it's a continual fight when you want to challenge what the service is doing. Institutionally, it's not only allowed but encouraged to propose new ideas and offer recommendations that may differ from the established path, but many leaders are risk averse and unwilling to support such actions. They don't want to go against the Army narrative. We eventually got these lessons out in the *Field Artillery Journal*, but not for over three years. I felt compelled to wait until I left the unit in 2019 to finally publish "Enhancing Rocket Artillery Certification with the Trainer Pod."

Feeling confident we had put the work into the technical aspects of firing rockets, I went to advocate for their use. My first test as the HIMARS liaison officer was at the weekly targeting meeting, a chance to represent my asset outside the strike cell and get rocket artillery into the fight. Nobody in attendance knew who I was, allowing me to sit back and observe, chiming in when appropriate. However, I quickly realized I was outside my comfort zone, so I relied much more on listening than participating, a challenging feat. Instead of presenting targets and debating strike options, which would have been my opportunity to sell HIMARS as an essential targeting tool, it was big-picture planning, a look ahead to the next few weeks of Iraqi movement, and an analysis of potential coalition support.

It was gibberish. Words like "Daesh" and "Kubaysah" seemed to have meant something to everyone in the room but me (Daesh is another term for ISIS, and Kubaysah was an Iraqi town that needed to be liberated, and soon was). Labels for Task Force This and Task Force That covered maps I didn't recognize, highlighting friendly forces in our general area. The colonel rambled on. I smiled and nodded, but I was lost in the situation's complexities and convinced there was no way everyone was following along perfectly. Then I remembered it was my first week, and the men and women in the room had been living this mission day in and day out for months.

The colonel walked the group through the upcoming Iraqi campaign, focusing on how we could shape the future urban battlefield for the Iraqi military with some preplanned strikes. Stated simply, we were assessing how to blow up any ISIS members in the next town before the Iraqi military arrived. The enemy would be easy to find as the coalition had already begun monitoring the city from above with drones. The biggest hurdle, he noted, was ammunition and available strike aircraft. While the drones were often armed, they were limited to Hellfire missiles. Although the Hellfire is an excellent munition, capable of striking moving targets with incredible precision, it lacks the destructive power to destroy buildings. Taking down an ISIS safe house or breaking up an indoor gathering required a bomb or, if I had anything to say about it, an M31 precision rocket from one of my HIMARS launchers.

The Ramadi campaign had strained resources. More importantly, it highlighted a significant aircraft shortfall for this type of warfare. Once a plane ran out of bombs, something that happened very quickly when you destroy entire city blocks, it became nothing more than an observation platform. While observation assets were abundant, lethality was limited, and only a few aircraft were dedicated to supporting ground operations at any given time. Once it released its bombs, an aircraft had to leave the area to reload. This time-consuming process would temporarily leave the strike cell without its most destructive assets. As the Iraqi military prepared to embark on a multi-town liberation campaign, this was a problem the coalition needed to address, a problem I had the answer to.

The colonel presented the issue to the group. Few provided solutions. Others complained that we should conduct fewer strikes, arguing that the Iraqis needed to rely less on coalition airpower. This was a narrative I grew to support, often wishing we would leave the Iraqis to fight their own war, come what may. After these comments were dismissed, the room fell silent for a minute, and I took the opportunity.

"We need to start using HIMARS for more strikes, especially on buildings," I chimed in, hoping to start a conversation. Instead, the colonel leaped on the idea. His eyes lit up. Validation. It was the answer he was looking for. He let us know he had recently sat down with some Air Force senior leaders at the Combined Air Operations Center, and they had reached similar conclusions. Looking back at the conversation, it made sense this was where he was attempting to steer the meeting, intending for us to arrive at the same conclusions he had. He thanked me for my answer, welcomed me as the new face of the meeting, and asked what my job was.

"I'm the HIMARS liaison officer, sir," I said proudly. A handful of people, including the colonel, started laughing.

"Of course you want more HIMARS," he said amid the laughter, "you're the rocket guy!" My answer was not any less valid because of my bias toward the system I represented, but it did carry less weight. It was a great icebreaker with the targeting team that worked outside the strike cell. Even if they didn't know my name, I was now "the rocket guy," a nickname assigned but not yet earned. However, if I was going to get my system in the fight, I needed to know what was happening. I needed to understand the bigger picture and how I fit into it. So, I stayed after the meeting to try to understand the game plan.

CHAPTER 8

The Game Plan

The plan didn't matter much if the Iraqis didn't execute it or refused to fight.

"I'm so fucking confused right now," I said after introducing myself to the other junior officers who lingered around the map as everyone left the targeting office. Before heading back to the strike cell, I took the opportunity to pick the brains of some of the brightest officers on the compound, the ones who had been planning the next offensive since the day Ramadi was liberated. I didn't know any of them personally, but I knew they had spent some long hours each day prepping for the upcoming campaign.

You could smell the hard work on them. Literally. This is another side effect of working in close quarters in the heat, in an environment with lunchtime workouts and an occasional missed shower. We all stank, yours truly included. That's an aspect of deployments often glossed over. With body odor, garbage everywhere, and the unique ways militaries dispose of shit, combat stinks, and you just have to get over it and adjust.

Smells aside, I needed to know more, and the small map room in the targeting directorate was the best place on the compound to gain the information I needed.

My lack of knowledge regarding the tactical situation with ISIS was embarrassing. While I had devoted most of my time to figuring out all the technical requirements of my job, I neglected the big picture understanding of the war and how my rocket-artillery missions would fit into the broader strategy. However, even as I began to grasp the larger campaign against ISIS over the course of my deployment, I still struggled to make sense of our missions. Instead, each rocket fired was nothing more than an individual moment in time, just another statistic I captured on a rather depressing Excel tracker.

After that first meeting, I decided I would never again be the dumb guy in the corner, afraid to speak, nodding and pretending I knew what was being discussed. I learned long ago I needed to understand the maneuver plan to integrate fire-support capabilities. Knowing what my system could do was a prerequisite for employing it effectively, but more was needed. I had to be able to communicate to everyone that there were times when it made the most sense to use rocket artillery for a mission. I needed to craft arguments explaining why we needed to save the few bombs we had on whatever aircraft was providing support. This required a detailed understanding of what the Iraqi military was doing, how the coalition intended to support it, and how each aspect of the operation fit into the larger mission.

To get to that level of understanding, I needed help. At the same time, I didn't want to embarrass myself in the strike cell with stupid questions, exposing my knowledge gap and allowing others to pounce on my weakness. From the outside looking in, the military officer community probably appears to be all smiles and pleasantries. But most of us know it's a savage community, a zero-sum game filled with people ready to climb over the backs of their peers to achieve personal success.

"We got you, bro. What's tripping you up?" one of them asked. Three or four captains around a map was a much-lower threat environment, and I felt more comfortable asking stupid questions and exposing my ignorance.

"Don't laugh, all of it," I replied. They laughed. But they were more than happy to get me up to speed, excited even that someone wanted to hear about all the work they had been doing. It took dramatically longer than it should have, but they were supportive, and we worked through it. The names of towns and friendly positions seemed to be in a foreign language, and the marker-scribbled tactical graphics may well have been hieroglyphics, but, at the same time, the experience was familiar. I knew the country and was comfortable just bullshitting with my peers around a map.

The situation wasn't as bad as I had imagined when I first landed in Iraq. The media has a way of making things seem worse than they are. At the same time, the Army often undersells the dangers of a mission to those undertaking it, highlighting successful operations but avoiding discussing its failures or the associated risks. The reality was somewhere between the scare tactics on the news and the pep talks I had received from my military leadership.

By February 2016, ISIS still controlled large areas in both Iraq and Syria, but Iraqi security forces had been making progress. Our mission, as we understood it, was the main effort in the coalition's three-pronged approach to defeating ISIS in Iraq.

First, the enemy had to be denied its ability to move freely between Iraq and Syria. Coalition air assets constantly patrolled the border area between the countries, interdicting any enemy cross-border traffic. This limited the number of reinforcements and resupply operations ISIS could conduct, reducing their ability to expand territory or fight a prolonged campaign. This mission was generally outside of our concern and often coordinated through special-operations forces. To be honest, I never followed what was going on in that wasteland. There was no need. I don't think anything happening near the border had an impact on our operations while I was there. As the saying goes, out of sight, out of mind.

Second, Iraqi security forces needed a secure central hub for theater-wide operations. To accomplish this meant expelling ISIS from central Iraq. This formed the core of our mission. If successful, it would open critical supply routes and enable the Iraqi military to synchronize its activities across the country. Securing central Iraq would have the secondary effect of ensuring the nation's capital didn't fall under ISIS control, collapsing the country into further chaos. Regional successes across Iraq would mean little if the black flag flew over Baghdad. Because of these factors, our mission was the main effort, at least while I was there.

Lastly, if the first two efforts were successful, we would effectively isolate ISIS in their Iraqi stronghold of Mosul. This would create an opportunity to destroy a large group of ISIS fighters or scatter their makeshift army. This battle eventually unfolded as one of the bloodiest of the war, with thousands of casualties on each side. In fact, for most military analysts studying the war, the battle to recapture Mosul would become the focal point of Operation *Inherent Resolve* research, consuming the preponderance of the literature on the conflict to date. However, the transition to northern Iraq and the battle for Mosul wouldn't occur while I was deployed. I had more pressing matters, and so did the Iraqi military.

Going into the meeting, I knew my mission was central Iraq, but I didn't know much about ISIS in the region or the coalition's plan to deal with it. I was surprised to discover a reasonably coherent campaign design, given the associated chaos of Operation *Inherent Resolve*. With the big picture out of the way, we got into the weeds, diving into the details of the upcoming Iraqi operations.

"Fallujah is everything," one said passionately. Bottom line up front—that is such an Army thing to do. When talking with a veteran, don't be discouraged if they are blunt and straight to the point. The military ingrains that into service members.

After Ramadi was retaken, the coalition effort shifted to isolating ISIS, who took refuge in Fallujah, creating a stronghold we would eventually have to deal with. The enemy had fortified the town and trapped 50,000 to 100,000 civilians inside; it was hard to get exact numbers. However, the Iraqi security forces were in no position to mount an offensive, at least not yet. Instead, the plan was to cut off all supplies and reinforcements into Fallujah, a modern-day siege that could last for months.

"Everything we're doing is a lead up to Fallujah. We can't just keep it isolated. Not for long anyway," he added.

The siege came with inherent risks to the civilians inside the city. There was a shared sentiment among the coalition officers that time was not on our side. We knew ISIS wouldn't grant people safe passage, nor would they share humanitarian aid with their captives. This strategy could lead to an international incident and tarnish the coalition narrative, undermining what little success we had achieved so far.

But the Iraqi leadership running the planning efforts didn't share our sense of urgency. In fact, they were in no hurry to conduct the assault on Fallujah. And who could blame them? Fallujah had proved a tough challenge for the US military a decade prior. The Iraqi military knew it would be a bloody battle, regardless of how much air support we provided. Our job, then, was to make mission success more likely, easing the burden the ground forces would face.

To soften Fallujah as a stronghold, we needed to weaken any fortifications and fighting positions in and around the town with air strikes. This would limit how much area ISIS could realistically defend, reducing its ability to repel the eventual offensive. We could also focus on making the objective area as small as possible by helping the Iraqis secure surrounding neighborhoods. If we were aggressive with our strike assets before an offensive, many of these smaller neighborhoods were likely to be abandoned, with ISIS fighters seeking refuge among civilians in the safety of Fallujah proper.

I added my two cents. "Got it. Fallujah's super important. It makes sense to me, it's the only town I've actually heard of." Then I did some quick math, laying my arm on the map as a poor-man's ruler. "Not to be 'that guy,' but that is way out of HIMARS range. When do we talk rockets?" Fallujah was well over one hundred kilometers from where my launchers were located at Al Asad, pretty much guaranteeing I wouldn't be a part of that battle.

That got a few laughs. "Fair enough," they started up again. "I think you'll be a lot more interested in the intermediate objectives." While important, the Fallujah fight was not the right-now mission. It would be some time before the conditions were right for such an attack. Instead, the initial operation the coalition would need HIMARS for was an assault on the district of Hit.

The Hit district was the only stronghold ISIS retained in central Iraq outside of Fallujah. This objective, a string of small towns, was much smaller and more manageable. The Iraqi offensive to retake the district was scheduled to begin in early March, giving me little time to get my team ready. Thousands of innocent civilians remained trapped inside the district's two main towns—Hit and Kubaysah.

Side note, I respect that the local Iraqis were not combatants in this situation, but I struggled to see them as innocent bystanders. Years of counter-insurgency operations and my personal dealings with the local populace five years prior skewed how I viewed them. They may not have been our enemy, but they weren't our friends either. They were partners of convenience, something that wouldn't last forever. Still, for now, they were clearly the victims.

The surrounding neighborhoods, on the other hand, were generally abandoned or repurposed by ISIS. Without the potential for civilian casualties, these areas became easy targets for coalition strikes.

The Hit district was dramatically closer to the HIMARS firing point at Al Asad Air Base than Fallujah or Ramadi. HIMARS missions into this district would range from 25 to 45 kilometers, the perfect range for precision rockets. In fact, it was so close that Iraqi security forces planned to use Al Asad as a staging base for their offensive and had already begun repositioning troops in preparation. But before they would start moving troops into the district, we needed to shape the area with strikes, reducing any defensive positions and breaking the will of the enemy fighters.

The Iraqi military was not looking for a fair fight. Actually, they weren't looking to fight at all. After seeing how poorly it had defended major cities like Ramadi, Fallujah, and Mosul against Islamic State, I wasn't sure how prepared their military was for the undertaking. Still, we were able to stack the odds in their favor. Coalition engagements with ISIS were incredibly lopsided. It was a technological mismatch, and if we could destroy the enemy before our teammates had to assume any risk, there would be no complaints from Iraqi military officers seeking some sort of glory.

Because of how close the Iraqi operations were to Al Asad, preparing the battlefield for the Hit offensive meant a chance to start shooting some rockets at the enemy. This was my opportunity to get HIMARS into the fight and do my part. If I played my cards right and demonstrated how well the systems could augment our limited aircraft, I would be very busy when the offensive began. I returned to the strike cell a new man, more excited than nervous; I was reinvigorated. My first mission was coming. It was finally time to do what I signed up for. I was going to kill the enemy with artillery fire.

CHAPTER 9

The Strike Cell

Our ragtag band of nerds dominated the battlefield.

"Looks like we've got something," the battle captain announced to the group. Side conversations stopped, and the small, dark room went silent, everyone in the strike cell waiting for the update. We were all anxious, maybe even excited.

The strike cell was built for efficiency and teamwork and was manned by no more than twenty people. Nobody held meetings there or briefed senior leaders except when gaining special permission to strike a sensitive target like a mosque. More on that adventure later. When visitors came, and plenty did, they found themselves standing awkwardly off to the side, viewing the team in action instead of receiving a presentation. If you didn't have a role, you didn't have a seat. There was little room for visitors, just a tiny area near the entrance by the coffee/snack table.

The strike cell had no dais or podium; it was a modern-day round table where everyone had a voice. But instead of a circle, three rows of seats faced a wall of ten flatscreen televisions stacked five abreast. Nine of these aired live drone and aircraft feeds from across Iraq. The real-time video allowed us to watch the war unfold in a way never before imagined.

The battle captain sat at the center of the room with his noncommissioned officer counterpart and a few enablers, occupying numerous seats in the second row. They were part of the Army division responsible for Iraq. More specifically, they were leaders from the division artillery headquarters. These artillery troops were the link between the strike cell and the rest of the division. They were also the group that worked with the higher headquarters that remained down in Kuwait, enabling final mission approvals.

After a few agonizing moments waiting for him to synthesize the updates he was receiving from our intelligence team in his chat, the battle captain looked up from his computer: "We tracked five males entering a building, all armed; initial assessment is a likely meeting to discuss the town's defenses." Iraqi military forces were preparing to move toward the town in the next few weeks; we all knew eliminating a group of enemy fighters for them was a high-priority mission, one that would be easy to get approved.

The war had begun again, and I sat quietly as an observer, finally ready to join in. The strike cell had prosecuted a couple of missions since I had arrived, but the targets were small, requiring only quick responses, usually Hellfire missiles fired from drones. These targets included enemy fighters stacking sandbags on rooftops to build fighting positions and ISIS cadre walking the streets with weapons slung on their backs. We were prepping the town for an eventual offensive by the Iraqi military by minimizing any ISIS resistance. Every mission was critical. With each enemy fighter we killed, we increased the Iraqi military's chances of success.

The mission that was developing was different than those minor engagements. This was going to be a large strike. We were going to destroy the building; there was no doubt about it. But, first, we needed to determine who would be privileged to lead the strike and gain all the associated glory that would follow. We all wanted to take the lead, creating a fun friendly rivalry as everyone vied for the director's ear.

The strike-cell director was a major who sat in the center of the top row with multiple liaisons on both sides. While a one-star general oversaw strike-cell operations and provided our necessary authorities as the target-engagement authority, a field-grade officer served as the director, coordinating the actions of the three rows into a single presentable strike proposal for the big boss. The general spent most of his time on the other side of the building in an Iraqi operations center, building partnerships and driving the Iraqi military to action when necessary. We quickly discovered the importance of his pressure on their military, as the Iraqis hesitated to commit to anything involving risk.

"All right, legal, are we good?" the director asked, turning his attention to our resident military lawyer, who had a permanent seat just to the left of the battle captain. It was a rotational position filled mainly by a Marine with whom I became friends during the deployment over a few hundred hours playing chess in our downtime. While strikes moved quickly from target identification to lethal prosecution, a deliberate approval process was still followed that didn't begin without clear legal justification. Everyone in the room became very comfortable explaining the situations we observed in the video feeds in terms of rules of engagement, framing every strike with legal jargon.

The lawyer blessed off before we fired any mission. If there was ever potential legal ambiguity, we adjusted the mission by changing the munition type or aim point, delaying the strike to gather more information, or, in rare instances, deciding not to prosecute at all. However, just because something is legal does not mean it's inherently right. This is an underlying challenge of this kind of technological warfare.

Most of the strike requests that reached our level were, legally, generally straightforward. This was the case with the five men with weapons. They were positively identified as enemy fighters, had gathered for a meeting, and chose to link up in a building in enemy occupied territory. Simple enough. The lawyer blessed off on our target analysis and the process began in earnest.

The strike director started the internal competition, a chance for the liaisons to fight for the right to run the mission. "All right, team, what are we thinking? Give me some options."

We had numerous strike assets at our fingertips for engaging the enemy. The first and simplest were the armed drones that dominated Iraqi airspace. These systems, which also served as our eyes across the country, often carried Hellfire missiles. Because they are laser guided, Hellfires are great for striking moving targets, but they don't cause much damage. This limited the types of targets we could use them against. For example, a Hellfire is perfect for engaging a motorcycle, rowboat, or an enemy fighter on the run. But if the target was in a building, the only way the missile could strike him was if the operator guided it through a window—not impossible, but unnecessarily complex.

It pains me to admit it, but aircraft were our most destructive asset. These platforms carried an assortment of 500-, 1,000-, and 2,000-pound bombs, all of which were more explosive than any rocket I could fire. If we needed to destroy a building, a large bomb would be the most straightforward solution and my biggest competition to getting my rockets into the fight. But that didn't stop me from arguing my case, which I always did nice and loud.

The last asset was mine. Rocket artillery.

Each rocket is equipped with three built-in fuzing options for varying mission types. The fuze is the rocket's tip; it explodes at a prescribed time or condition, engaging the rocket's effects at different points of its flight. Point detonation is the standard fuze, meaning the rocket explodes upon contacting its target. An example target for this fuze is a parked vehicle, with the rocket exploding the instant it strikes the vehicle.

The second option is a delay fuze, allowing the rocket to penetrate a target one meter before exploding. Delay fuzes are generally for buildings, creating an internal explosion versus a surface one. Stated another way, the rocket relies on its speed to crash through the roof of a building. After burrowing inside, the fuze detonates, destroying a room and killing everyone in it or destroying an intermediate level of a two-story structure instead of just blowing a big hole in the roof. This fuze is essential for limiting collateral damage in an urban environment. This was the fuze we used most often when firing rocket artillery into the cities of Iraq. Throughout the deployment, we tried to use this method to kill the building's occupants without destroying the structure.

The final fuze is a proximity fuze, which relies on an internal sensor to explode the rocket roughly ten meters above the designated target zone. When the rocket detonates from this height, it rains lethal shrapnel down on enemy forces. This is the best fuze for engaging a group of people out in the open, a fuze designed for killing humans en masse. While we rarely had opportunities to employ this fuze type in the urban conflict, it proved its worth when we did.

We all knew a large bomb from an aircraft was the director's preference. I hadn't been in the fight yet. I hadn't proved myself or my capability. It wasn't a fair competition. At least not initially.

"ALO, when's the next bird checking on?" the director asked.

The Air Force dominated the first row with air-liaison officers (ALO) and joint terminal attack controllers. These highly trained specialists maintained a direct connection with the manned fighters in the region, providing technical expertise and, when directed, the terminal control of aircraft that gave pilots their attack guidance and approval for drops.

Right next to them sat an airspace-management warrant officer who operated arguably our most crucial piece of equipment, the tactical airspace integration system, commonly referred to as the TAIS and, like most of the Army's acronyms, is pronounced as a word, "tay-iss." This TAIS computer allowed us to manage the airspace in the region, which is fundamental for all strikes and is one of the most significant challenges in this kind of warfare. Iraqi airspace was chaos, crowded by the combination of commercial aircraft and coalition strike platforms like fighter jets and drones. In turn, convincing the team to let me shoot 13-foot-long rockets through that congestion was always an interesting conversation. My rockets added confusion, and the process was inherently slow and difficult, requiring careful airspace management.

"Sorry, sir, nothing for another few hours," the air liaison responded.

My lucky day. We had no manned aircraft overhead that morning, and none were expected until after lunch.

The strike director pondered the situation and looked down his row. Two liaison teams sat to the director's left. The first, a special-operations liaison, provided unique insights into land forces in the area, leveraging connections with other special-operation advisors throughout the country. This was essential for determining the truth behind Iraqi military reporting. Too often, during an offensive operation, the Iraqi commander on the ground would inflate the enemy's capabilities or provide misleading information if it painted his unit in a positive light. Having a trusted agent from the special-operations community in a position to relay information or confirm battlefield details allowed us to overcome conflicting information and avoid getting bogged down in the fog of war.

The second liaison team coordinated the flight and execution of armed drones in the area, communicating with drone pilots worldwide who operated equipment in our area of responsibility. Drones were our foundation for targeting. Because coalition forces didn't conduct patrols with Iraqi security forces, we had to rely on drone technology to identify targets, validate target location data, observe the impacts, and perform a battle-damage assessment after each strike. Our drone liaison enabled the strike cell by rapidly repurposing these drones based on internal intelligence assessments or Iraqi reporting.

The last seat was mine, a corner spot on the director's right side. It was a dark corner, positioned directly under the air conditioner, but too close to the wall to actually feel the cool air as it blasted over my head to the next row. And right next to an old refrigerator that was a relic from another era, covered in dings and scratches. It looked, and sounded, like it had been struggling to fight the Iraqi heat for decades. I was hidden away, out of sight … but I wouldn't be out of mind. I would be loud, I would be heard, and I would be in the fight.

Without an aircraft overhead and our drones unable to prosecute such a large target, rockets became a viable option.

The strike director looked my way with a toothy grin, and my heart started racing. "Looks like the new guy is getting in the fight today," he announced to the group. "Let's see what you and those rockets you won't shut up about can do."

My heart nearly leaped from my chest. I tried to speak, but it was like I had cotton in my mouth. I nodded instead of talking and started mentally running through my fire-mission drills. This was no practice mission, however. This mission would end in the death of our enemies. I was about to do something I would never forget. I was about to launch rockets. I was about to take another life. And I was ecstatic.

CHAPTER 10

Splash!

We did evil things, but we did them to evil men.

We pulled the drone's video feed onto one of our televisions and examined the building. These screens enabled us to find and track the enemy. Our role was to serve as the judge and jury, deciding their fate. If we chose to act, the televisions offered front-row seats to the subsequent executions. The video feeds were recorded and often shared with leaders across the theater as success stories, reminders to those in supporting roles of the effectiveness of coalition operations. The last television was for entertainment and generally bounced between news and sports, with a surprising amount of professional wrestling. To be perfectly honest, the other nine were often pretty entertaining to watch as well.

Step one was to make sure the launchers and the crews were prepared to receive the mission. While they lived in a constant state of readiness, they were by no means sitting in their vehicles waiting for action. I had chat software on my regular laptop to enable mission coordination and provide fire commands. This allowed me to open a conversation with the rest of my HIMARS team—both at the firing point and, if needed, down in Kuwait—to validate all mission data and eventually provide the commands to move to the firing point, fire the mission, and move back to the staging area. I hopped into our chat room and let the fire-direction center know a mission was coming their way and it wasn't an exercise.

I later discovered this software was also my venue for coordinating mission information with other supporting forces in the area. For example, a subordinate headquarters would contact me directly to see if the HIMARS at the firing point was busy or available for a potential mission. On occasion, I would have direct conversations with one of the drone technicians, mainly when they were conducting damage assessments for HIMARS strikes.

Ready or not, it was my time to shine.

I took over the strike cell. "Chief, can you drop a rough grid? It doesn't have to be perfect. I just need the launchers to pull some data."

We would clean it up later while playing the waiting game, an accepted eventuality in this environment. I only needed the initial grid to be accurate enough to start planning airspace deconfliction. I sent the grid to the firing point, and we split our efforts. The fire-direction center at Al Asad alerted the launcher crews and started computing the fire-mission data.

"Dropping airspace data in the group chat now," I announced it to everyone, but it was primarily for our airspace manager. Whenever possible, we posted information where everyone could see it. The more eyes that saw the information, the less likely a mistake would go unnoticed. A mistake when firing rockets or dropping bombs could prove quite costly, both in innocent lives and the overall coalition narrative, not to mention the career of those responsible.

I provided our airspace manager with the three things he needed for our mission: the location the unit would fire from, the location of the target, and the maximum altitude the rocket would reach in flight. With this information, he requested a "hotwall" airspace-coordination measure to clear all nearby aircraft from the rocket's calculated path for the upcoming fire mission. This is essentially a massive imaginary wall from the launcher to the target, in this case, roughly fifty kilometers long, which no aircraft could cross unless it flew at very high altitudes. With the airspace-deconfliction process underway, which we quickly discovered was generally the most time-consuming aspect, we began weaponeering the mission. Yes, "weaponeering" is a real word. More on that in a minute.

"Chief, I'm coming down to you. You got the screens up?" I looked over our targeting warrant officer's shoulders. He had the building displayed on his computer with split images showing different angles.

Our targeting warrant officer had special software for producing target coordinate mensuration, which is just a fancy way of saying extremely accurate grid coordinates for rockets and bombs. The software is called the Precision Strike Suite Special Operations Forces and is also referred to as PSS-SOF. It's pronounced "Piss-Off." I'm trying to avoid using too many acronyms, but that one is too good not to share.

We looked at the building together, pondering a potential firing plan. It was a simple square structure that appeared to be a residence, mostly a single story, with a small section elevated to two levels. Most fire-mission processes are technical and can be done by following a script. These actions can be considered the science of warfare. In contrast, weaponeering is fluid, a conversation about how we understand the problem and what we believe is the best solution. This is the art of warfare, something I worked to continually improve on.

Weaponeering is a three-step process. The first step is to determine which strike asset to use. In this case, with no aircraft nearby to drop a bomb, rockets were the obvious course of action if we wanted the building destroyed. Plus, the director had already made his choice. This wasn't always the case. As often as not, the air-liaison officer and I would simultaneously devise plans to destroy the target with our assets. We would then pitch our respective approaches, also known as target solutions, to the director. He would make the final decision on what weapon system we would use. This created a fun rivalry.

I constantly fought to prove how effective Army rocket artillery was, embracing my role as "the rocket guy." But this was often an uphill battle as the capabilities aircraft brought to the fight were well-known and widely appreciated. In contrast, few people were very familiar with rockets. What knowledge people did have was generally wrong or outdated information based on the role of rocket artillery during *Desert Storm*. My rockets were awesome, but they were not the grid-square killers of the past. This is a knowledge gap I sought to remedy then and have continued since.

Once an asset is selected, the next step is to choose how many different targets and aimpoints are needed to sufficiently destroy the target.

"What are you thinking?" I asked, looking at the imagery with our targeting officer. "Three? That should ensure we get that second story part."

"Makes sense to me," he replied.

We settled on a three-rocket solution, making a triangle of aim points on the building's roof. While neither of us had any engineering training or architecture knowledge, our chosen spots seemed like logical structural points to bring about the building's demise. We were artists, leveraging our experiences versus relying on some software or checklist, with each mission providing new data points to draw from.

The final step is fuzing. We selected options to ensure the strike had the desired effects. This was a straightforward mission. Each rocket would use a delay fuze, penetrating through the roof and detonating a meter inside the building.

Each aimpoint was then input into software that allowed us to view collateral-damage estimates for a potential target with varying munition types. While we accepted the building the enemy fighters were occupying needed to be destroyed, we did our best to limit that destruction. It made the strikes more palatable for senior leaders. We used the software to produce graphical representations of a likely blast radius. The final product was a circle on a PowerPoint slide superimposed on satellite imagery. Although only a prediction, this picture provided a pretty accurate estimate of the extent of damage different munitions would have.

Once we were complete and satisfied collateral damage was minimized, we sent a screenshot of this graphic to the higher headquarters command down in Kuwait. It provided the visual basis for requesting the final authorization to strike, highlighting what impacts, if any, a proposed strike would have on surrounding infrastructure. Because of the emphasis on limiting collateral damage, we would sometimes select suboptimal solutions to ensure mission approval. That wasn't a problem this time. In fact, it generally wasn't a problem at all when using rockets.

With the firing solution agreed upon, I built the mission into the artillery computer and sent it to the firing point. We opted to use both launchers, two rockets from one and one rocket from the other. By having the first two rockets hit at the same time then followed by the third, instead of three consecutively, we increased the destructive capacity of the initial blast, limiting the enemy's reaction time and decreasing the chances anyone could survive. While not this day, I would soon discover that some people just refused to die.

The HIMARS crews loaded into their vehicles, and the fire-direction center sent me back mission-confirmation data over our chat on the other computer. By validating the grid coordinates and mission instructions over two systems, we created an internal redundancy to identify potential mistakes. The rocket would strike whatever grid we programmed into it if it was within its range. The last thing we wanted to do was fire one of these munitions at the wrong place because one of us input the location data incorrectly. A small typo could cost people their lives and end a lot of our careers. We had rehearsed enough to be confident. It was time, and we were ready.

The director alerted the general, and we quickly ran him through the plan. All parties involved briefed him on the necessary details, such as the legal justification for conducting the strike and how we were mitigating unnecessary collateral damage. This was my first opportunity to brief him in a formal setting. I explained our weaponeering solution, and he looked to our targeting officer for validation. When briefing senior leaders, ensuring everyone's on the same page beforehand is wise. The last thing he needed to see was us debate the technical minutia of the mission. This was one of the reasons why we created the target solution proposal as a team. The targeting officer was my partner in developing the plan, so he obviously agreed with the assessment.

"All right, do it," the general said, approving the mission and allowing us to move forward. "I'm pulling up a seat for this one. Let's see it, rocket guy."

The mission data was all relayed to the theater headquarters in Kuwait for any last-minute issues and final approval. My adrenaline started pumping. There was no turning back. While our second-row team radioed to Kuwait, I ordered the launchers to move to the firing point.

It was only a short distance between the staging area and the firing point, but it was important to refrain from firing missions from next to where people lived. The enemy threat may have been minimal, but HIMARS was a valuable target incredibly easy to identify when it launched its large rockets. Even without using some expensive radar system, enemy forces could identify the launch because the rocket leaves a lingering trail of smoke from its origin that can be seen from far away. It might not have been a fair fight, but if enemy forces fired back, mortar rounds landing on the barracks where people were sleeping would be the worst-case scenario.

Our higher headquarters gave the final approval, and the launchers reported they were at the firing point, standing by for my command to fire.

"Launchers are at the firing point," I echoed the report to the group. "How are we coming on airspace? Are we clear?" I asked loud enough for the whole strike cell to hear. Airspace wasn't clear. Spoiler, it wouldn't be clear for a while.

Hurry up and wait, the story of so many military operations. While we may have moved through our procedures effectively and positioned the HIMARS to strike, that aspect of the process was never what prevented us from firing promptly.

We waited. Then we waited some more. Continual status updates from our airspace manager reiterated we were almost there and that it should only take another minute. And then we waited some more. "Should" is a terrible planning word.

We weren't good at clearing airspace this way. While we had practiced the air-deconfliction procedures, we underestimated the time it would take to get all the aircraft out of the way. This was something we would have to address moving forward. After the umpteenth status check, our airspace manager gave the green light that the airspace was clear, and my heart started racing.

"Sir?" I looked to the director for final confirmation, letting him know all the conditions were met for a safe strike and that the launchers were ready to fire. He gave the approval, and I typed the order to fire into the computer.

"Shot!" I yelled it dramatically louder than I probably needed to, silencing any chatter in the strike cell and informing everyone the HIMARS crew had fired the first rocket. I owned the room for a brief moment, and all eyes turned to the television with the feed, ready to finally see HIMARS in action.

"All rockets successfully fired!" I said at a much more reasonable volume a few seconds after the third rocket was fired.

We added that additional update to let everyone know the firing process was complete and that there weren't any issues. A misfire with a 13-foot-long rocket is a big deal and potentially deadly for the crew. If, for example, the rocket engine ignited, but the rocket failed to launch and instead was stuck in its pod, then the HIMARS crew—unable to immediately evacuate—would be stuck with unexploded ordnance on the top of their truck. I joke about how these precision rockets were designed for smaller explosions compared to bombs, but having one ready to explode on the roof of your truck is a situation nobody wants to be in. Luckily, we never ran into this issue.

Then, the fun part: more waiting. After staring at the television for a few seconds, the general asked half-jokingly, "When are things going to start exploding, Brennan?" It would be dramatically longer than he expected. Everyone in the strike cell had become comfortable with the immediate results that came from dropping bombs and firing Hellfire missiles; rockets took a hell of a lot longer. There was no instant gratification.

"About two minutes, sir," I replied. Two very long and stressful minutes. The rockets flew very fast but had a lot of ground to cover. Plus, they have to climb to a high altitude, allowing the rocket to strike with a near-vertical descent. It was clear from his facial expression this was not what he wanted to hear.

Most people returned to what they were doing, ready to give the screen their undivided attention right before the impact. They wouldn't share my anxiety as each second ticked slowly down.

Less than thirty seconds into the rocket's flight, one of the ISIS fighters stepped out of the building and started looking around.

"Looks like you're only getting four today," someone hollered from the first row.

There was no way to tell if the enemy fighter was looking for other companions that had not yet arrived, was just getting some fresh air, or if something in his gut told him to leave, to run. Something came over me. Caught up in the moment, I lost it and screamed at the monitor. In the process, I strung together an assortment of words I would later be told was "inappropriate" and "unprofessional" language.

It's a strange thing to be a purveyor of violence and destruction but not be allowed to curse. We were there to take another man's life, but we were forced to be gentlemen about it. This was a challenge for me almost daily.

It was weird how mad I got seeing someone leave the building. I guess I was selfish. I wanted all five of them. For someone to escape would be a failure, diminishing the mission's success. My goal was to fire as many rockets and kill as many ISIS members as possible.

Lucky for me—although somewhat dark in reflection now that I write it—and very unlucky for him, the lone straggler went back inside the building with little time to spare before the first rockets would impact, unwittingly sealing his fate.

"Splash!" I screamed, regaining everyone's attention. In the excitement, I was back to poor volume control, a pretty regular occurrence for me. This artillery command lets everyone know the explosion is about to happen. We calculate the flight time for every fire mission down to the second. Knowing that information, the fire-direction center (in this case, me) can alert the mission's observer (in this case, the entire strike cell) that rounds will impact in five seconds with the announcement of "splash." In a tactical scenario, this allows an observer to seek cover from hostile forces, only having to expose themselves to potential hostile fire right before friendly artillery rounds impacted. For this mission, I just wanted to remind everyone of the upcoming explosion and get their eyes back on the television screen before the impact. I wanted them to see how effective HIMARS rockets were.

The strike cell was silent, everyone watching the screen for the fireworks. I was giddy. I had worked for years, and this was it. I would finally do what I had trained for. I would finally kill the enemy. I was on my feet. Ready. I felt a chill run down my spine and shivered. At first, I thought it was nerves. Then I realized my "Spidey Sense" wasn't tingling; I was standing directly in the path of our air-conditioning unit that normally blasted right over my seat. It was the first time I felt the cool breeze.

Five seconds passed. Nothing happened. "Fuck, fuck, fuck," the words were barely audible but still enough to get the director's attention. He was not pleased with how I talked. This would be an enduring problem as long as we were desk mates.

Tick, tick, tick. Nothing. More of that "inappropriate" language left my mouth a whole lot louder as I tried to understand where my rockets went and why this building was not exploding. Scenarios ran through my head, and I couldn't help thinking I had somehow made a costly mistake that would likely end my career. I was exposed as a fraud. I had failed. I was filled with self-doubt. I couldn't believe it. And on my very first mission, no less.

Fun fact: it turns out that when someone says, "live feed," they mean it's not broadcasting something previously recorded. It doesn't mean the feed in question is transmitted instantaneously. In this case, there was about a fifteen-second delay between what the drone was observing and what was displayed in the strike cell. A very long 15 seconds.

And then it happened, and it was glorious.

"Holy shit!" someone yelled. "I saw the rockets perfectly." While the rockets went incredibly fast, we could see them fall from the sky and smash through the roof of the building. It was quite a sight. While there are always a few meters of potential error with the guided rockets, it was not a factor in this case. They were right on target, striking the programmed coordinates precisely. The strike cell erupted in cheers, me included.

"I only saw two," someone added. The first two arrived at the same time, or as close as my eyes could tell, and the third was barely three seconds behind it. "Never mind, there it is."

I didn't know what I expected to see as the observer of my first mission. I assumed the building would suddenly explode, a fireball like someone had planted a bunch of explosives on the inside that went off without warning. Maybe it would have been a cooler sight if I was actually out on the street instead of in my cozy little building. While watching these drone feeds, there was no sound, just visuals, drastically reducing the intensity of the experience. Because of this, the whole mission was muted, apart from our chatter.

The internal explosion created some interesting effects. Debris blasted out of windows and doorways. But these weren't chunks of the building. Instead, the pressure sent smaller items, fragments of furniture, and smoke out into the street. If there were humans in those rooms, they died instantly. The building came down on itself shortly after the third rocket impacted. A successful implosion. Collateral damage wasn't just minimal for this mission, it was nonexistent.

We watched the building for a few minutes. There was nothing. Nobody emerged, no rubble shifted, and no other groups in the area rushed to help. It was a perfect mission. The observer team posted the battle-damage assessment: "Building Destroyed, five enemies killed," the battle captain announced to the team.

"End of Mission," I announced, and relayed the information to the firing point and ordered the launchers to return to the staging area.

It's strange how we treat death. Sitting in our office, we were removed from our actions, at least to an extent. This was true even for the launchers. Firing the mission from more than thirty kilometers away, those soldiers would never see the enemy or the effects of their strike without someone sharing a video. Most of the time, they weren't even told what the target was. Instead, I would just issue fire commands for them to follow. These missions weren't up for debate, at least not at the firing point.

The mood in the strike cell wasn't somber after the mission. There was no stopping to reflect on the gravity of our decisions that morning or to take a moment to honor the dead. It was the opposite. Spirits were high, and we celebrated. We were proud of our ability to conduct the mission successfully, happy to see the enemy removed from the battlefield and, in general, we were a group of people who cheered when things went boom.

I thought my first fire mission would change everything, that it would be a defining moment in my life. I was surprised at how easy it was to take a life. How easy it was to kill another human being. Not technologically, pulling a trigger or flipping a switch isn't difficult. I thought I would have to deal with it emotionally. But there was no weight to it, no burden ... at least not initially. Maybe it would have been different if I found myself looking at dead bodies strewn about the street instead of a bunch of rubble. I knew the bodies were in there. I knew what we did. But I didn't have to face it like I thought I would.

Still, that day in 2016, the first time I killed the enemy, is a day I will never forget. It was my brother's birthday. I couldn't tell him about the strike, not yet anyway. Since then, when I have sent him that "Happy Birthday" text, or been a good brother and actually picked up the phone, I am also reminded of an important anniversary; I am reminded of the first time I helped take another person's life.

The mission was a team process, but I quarterbacked that one, and congratulations followed. It was a good feeling. I wanted more, much more. I created an Excel spreadsheet to track my missions. I updated it that day: three rockets fired, one building destroyed, and five enemies killed. I planned to fill that spreadsheet with the highest body count possible.

I'm sorry to share that goal; I'm sorry to have had it. But it's essential to understand how we thought about our actions and measured our success. The rational me knows it's wrong to measure success in death, to have the desire to kill the enemy even if they posed no immediate threat to us. Still, it was how I felt at the time. It's what it means to do the job, and I always strive to be the best at what I do. I'm not ashamed to take pride in my work or be proud of my team's success, but the approach may have been misguided.

It took some post-deployment reflection, some time away from the day-to-day life of the strike cell, to come to terms with the fact that the way we celebrated our missions and joked about the carnage is not how we should treat the act of taking another's life. These men were doing evil things, and I'm comfortable with the fact that they needed to die. I'm even okay that I was the one to do it. I'm disappointed I took pleasure in taking their lives, though, even if I wasn't alone. This was the norm, at least initially. I think we all changed how we viewed these missions throughout the deployment, just at different times or, for some, afterward upon reflection.

Still, on this day, I was proud. I had accomplished a professional goal. More importantly, we had a proof of concept for getting rocket artillery into the fight. HIMARS had the potential to support the upcoming Iraqi campaign. It was accurate, destructive, and produced minimal collateral damage. I was going to get very busy, and I let my varying bosses know it, hoping they would open the floodgates with ammunition. To my frustration, they didn't.

I felt the general's hand on my shoulder after the celebration died down. "Nice work, kid. But we need to get better. I'm going to need you to be a whole lot faster when we retake Kubaysah."

He was right. While the mission was successful, it was slow. Our fire-mission processing would have to be dramatically faster to support maneuvering forces on the ground. Moving forward, we would require the authority to drop buildings quickly coupled with a more effective airspace-clearance approach.

CHAPTER 11

Big Sky, Little Bullet

I'm shooting this shit; tell the pilots to clear the damn sky.

"That could have gone better," I told our airspace manager, initiating a difficult conversation. I commandeered a chair in the first row and sat down, ready to learn. We needed to work out the kinks. The way we were clearing airspace was not going to work. Not if we needed to strike the target quickly.

"Don't beat yourself up," he replied with a big smile. "You hit the target, and your little rockets made a decent explosion."

I stared at him blankly for a moment. "I'm talking about the thirty minutes it took for you to clear the airspace. That can't be the norm." He knew.

"I know," he said, easily as frustrated as I was. "It's a process. And it's a lot more complicated than you think it is. I can't just make everyone clear a path the instant you want to shoot."

"Not with that attitude you can't," I joked, lightening the mood. "Talk me through it. I don't get what the issue is and won't until I see what you see."

We were terrible at managing our airspace, at least initially. We were slow, reactive, and less situationally aware of potential hurdles before they arose. While this was generally just a minor inconvenience for the fixed-wing aircraft and drones providing support, our inefficiency was devastating to the integration of rocket artillery. If HIMARS weren't timely, rocket artillery wouldn't be relevant during the upcoming Hit offensive.

I could still conduct some deliberate strikes, destroying a random vehicle or an abandoned building. However, my system would be a last resort for more dynamic targets. I needed a better answer to the airspace-deconfliction issue to effectively employ my rockets and be a contributing member of the strike cell for the short window in which my team was involved in operations. I knew future campaigns like the liberation of Fallujah would fall well outside my range ring. When the Hit offensive ended and the effort shifted to Fallujah, rocket artillery would no longer be much of a factor, at least not in central Iraq.

We all knew, no matter what fixes we came up with, it would always remain a timely process to clear airspace for HIMARS. But I was determined to not let slow procedures cost us a mission. Selfishly, I wanted to fire every mission I could and rack up those statistics. Still, before I could lend a hand in fixing the problem, I needed to understand what our airspace manager requested and how the process worked.

"For the dynamic targets, I'm taking your firing data and just building a hotwall," he explained.

"Tracking. A big-ass ROZ from the launchers to the target," I replied. The ROZ, or restricted operating zone, is the control measure that prohibits the entry of any aircraft without coordination, allowing us to fire our rockets without risking one accidentally flying into an aircraft. While the probability of that happening is minuscule, pilots are not keen on a 13-foot-long rocket sharing their airspace, which makes sense.

"Kind of," he responded. I saw the look on his face. He was about to dumb this down for the artillery guy. "Think of it more like a dumbbell than a wall, with three separate chunks of airspace. That's something you should relate to." While hurtful, I do look like a meathead, so I couldn't be too mad.

He continued: "Imagine two large areas at the ends covering the firing point and target area with a skinnier strip between these two points, connecting them. Plus, the ROZ has to cover the area from the ground up to the rocket's maximum altitude, which is surprisingly high. It's a ton of airspace to simply shut down."

"Fair. Can you pull up the one you made for the last mission?" I asked. I understood the general process but wanted him to walk me through the mission to better grasp the nuances and see where we could potentially make some adjustments.

He nodded and displayed it on the screen. It was easy for him to do.

"Bro! That is massive!" I was shocked when he showed me the "hotwall" overlayed onto the map. It was enormous, with ridiculous measurements designed to be overly safe.

I was tracking how long it would be (the range of the mission) and how high (a little higher than my maximum calculated altitude), but the width was unexpected, consuming the map. The standard the strike cell was using for the radius of the hotwall ROZ at the firing point and target area was four to six miles and about half as wide for the flight path. These measurements varied slightly depending on which of our airspace-management crews was on shift, but every example he showed me was incredibly large.

The airspace-management team justified this enormous area by arguing it was safer for the pilots, ensuring manned aircraft were never within two miles of one of my rockets, an absurdly safe distance. Additionally, they explained that these measurements were what they were familiar with from their pre-deployment training. Still, this amount of airspace took way too long to coordinate, potentially upwards of 30 minutes as I discovered on some frustrating occasions. It was also too restrictive for other airspace users. With this design, an active hotwall would significantly limit air traffic in central Iraq, reducing its viability as a tool.

The simplicity of the hotwall made it the most straightforward solution. But this didn't mean it was the best. The time required to coordinate the airspace-control measure limited our responsiveness, and the amount of restricted flight area weakened the coalition's ability to conduct other essential air functions.

We did three things to overcome this challenge and speed up the process. First, we made the area as small as possible while still being able to accomplish the mission safely. As confidence grew in the precision of rocket artillery, the size of the ROZ gradually decreased, eventually only requiring a one-nautical-mile ROZ over the launcher and target area, with a mile-and-a-half wide strip connecting them. The decrease in size freed up more airspace for aircraft to use and dramatically reduced the time required to establish the ROZ.

The second thing we did was establish a system that enabled controlled entry of aircraft into the ROZ. All strikes were centrally managed, meaning the release approval of weapons from an aircraft came from the same strike cell where my HIMARS missions were being processed. Because of this, once a hotwall was established, the air-liaison officer could allow entry of local aircraft into the restricted zone as long as there was no upcoming artillery mission. This meant we could work closely together to allow a fighter or a drone to strike a target or conduct a quick reconnaissance mission. Once the aircraft left the ROZ, another "airspace clear" announcement was required before I would fire a mission; the last thing anyone wanted was to hurl a 13-foot-long rocket into occupied airspace and endanger one of our pilots or even the drones, no matter how unlikely a collision was. This method allowed for joint attacks on large structures and targets with numerous aim points that needed to be engaged at the same time. More importantly, it allowed me to control the airspace for a longer period of time without limiting our other strike capabilities.

Our final fix was to plan airspace measures in advance. This was easy when we could plan targets multiple days out, as most missions involved destroying a building. We attempted to make this airspace-control measure more technical through an approach called a "goalpost." This method decreased the airspace required to operate but was more complicated. Instead of making a wall, the goalpost was three boxes that formed an arch, leaving room for an aircraft to fly under the rocket's flight path. The most challenging part of this method was convincing pilots from varying nations that it was safe to pass under a fired rocket. The unsubstantiated fear a rocket might unexpectedly plummet from the sky at any given moment made this coordination less about creating an airspace-control measure and more about marketing awareness. Needless to say, we hardly used this method except for deliberately planned targets.

When the target was unknown, as was generally the case for day-to-day operations, planning massive airspace measures in advance was more complicated. But that didn't mean we couldn't do it; we just had to get creative. Our primary approach for doing this was to establish a pre-planned hotwall that extended from our firing point into a suspected enemy target zone. Because of our limited knowledge of enemy positions, we turned the hotwall into a large cone to cover the suspected area instead of making the standard dumbbell. By having the ROZ begin at the firing point and extend from a five to twenty-degree angle, we could cover a relatively large chunk of land in a targeted zone. While we couldn't hold this much airspace for too long, even with controlled entry, it allowed us to be responsive when the Iraqi military conducted a scheduled offensive.

This was precisely what we did during the Iraqi military's first major operation of the year, the Hit Offensive. Our target zone was a large neighborhood already assessed as having no civilians in the area, allowing us to destroy whatever buildings we deemed necessary. We used the neighborhood's main north–south road as a natural divider, planning to engage any targets west of the road with HIMARS and east of the road with aircraft. We kept our pre-planned hotwall active for over two hours during the opening of this operation as Iraqi forces entered the neighborhood, using the cone to cover the entire section of the targeted zone west of the road. This technique rapidly expedited the fire-mission process, culminating with a HIMARS mission that supported troops in contact.

It never took long for the Iraqi military to run into problems. This offensive faltered just after the Iraqi military forces entered a neighborhood under the umbrella of my hotwall airspace measure. Our Iraqi military partners were pinned down in the street, concentrating a surprising amount of firepower on a single building. They weren't advancing. If anything, they looked like they would pull back, like they were going to quit. We watched, frustrated at what looked like a mission on the cusp of failure.

Our US Army representative from the Iraqi operations center barged in, the connecting door just to the right of the televisions. "Apparently there's a machine-gun team in that small building," he reported, giving us the update secondhand. "We can't get them moving, can you guys take it out?" We all knew that operations wouldn't continue until it was destroyed. This was why the strike cell existed, but it was still frustrating.

I understand the desire to want to avoid taking risks; many Iraqi soldiers would likely die if that unit stormed the machine-gun position. It's natural. Why put your life in danger if you don't have to? To quote Homer Simpson's fantastic and winning political slogan: "Can't someone else do it?" Let someone else do the hard work, the dangerous work. Who can blame the Iraqi military for allowing the coalition to flex its might against ISIS? I always felt better during my patrols through Baghdad on my first deployment when we had helicopters overhead or nearby. Was their reliance on us so different?

But it was more than just receiving assistance; this was dependency. I knew the Iraqis weren't the great military we propped them up to be, but it was still surprising to see such a superior force struggle (more on this later). This was the first time I saw them in battle, and it was evident our "partners" had become reliant on Western technology to survive. What would that mean when we left again?

In their defense, we were enablers. The coalition quickly said "yes" when the Iraqi military asked for help. They had leverage; their bargaining chip was inaction, something the coalition wouldn't accept. So, when they asked for help, the strike director ordered us to destroy the building and neutralize the ISIS machine-gun nest.

"Too easy, let's take it out and get their offensive back on track," the director said, looking my way. Because the target was on the west side of our divider road, we didn't have to compete over who would get the mission. I was in the fight.

"Roger, sir. Sending the launchers the heads up and having them move to the firing point. Chief, simple mission, I'm thinking two rockets near the center, can you get me some refined grids?" We were moving quickly because we had done all the preparation work ahead of time—airspace was already deconflicted, the neighborhood was screened for civilian occupants, our delivery method was established by target location, and the authority to strike in support of the offensive had been delegated to our director.

"Launchers are moving to the firing point," I announced to the group. Our targeting officer dropped the updated grid coordinates in the group chat. "Sending the fire mission down to my guys. How are we on airspace?"

"We're good. Hotwall is still in place. No issues," our airspace manager said with a big smile. He wasn't holding up the process.

"Great work, team! Brennan, fire when ready," the director announced, giving the final approval.

The mission went off without a hitch. The two rockets landed simultaneously, and the building collapsed, silencing the machine gun for good and enabling the Iraqi military to continue the operation.

Our adjustments worked perfectly. These airspace-management techniques made employing HIMARS dramatically more straightforward and, more importantly, faster. We had adapted. In doing so, we became more efficient killers, something we were all pretty proud of. We needed to teach our teammates how to do the same and share these concepts with the entire force. To reach the widest audience, I captured our airspace lessons in the *Field Artillery Journal*—albeit in a much more technical fashion than explained here. Importantly, nobody tried to censor the piece this time. It was a good news story and wouldn't ruffle any feathers. In fact, it made our commander look good, as I am sure he took a lot of the credit with leaders back in the States.

With our new tactics, techniques, and procedures, we could request airspace faster and maintain it longer. We developed a relationship with our Air Force counterparts to get HIMARS more involved in the war. Moving forward, HIMARS missions were going to be simpler. Well, most of them, anyway.

CHAPTER 12

A Sanctuary No Longer

Nothing was off limits. It was a war zone, after all.

"The Iraqis are asking us to strike it, protective status be damned!" an Army colonel yelled as he burst into the strike cell.

It didn't come as much of a surprise. We had been watching the Iraqi advance on multiple screens. We saw their failure, and it was hard to ignore their casualties. ISIS fighters had established a fighting position in an unexpected building and were defending the hell out of it.

"All right, team, who wants to be the one to destroy a mosque?" the director asked.

This one was outside our comfort zone. Regardless of how fast our techniques allowed us to operate, this mission would take time. It didn't matter that the Iraqis requested the strike; it would be easy for the enemy to craft a damning narrative and turn a necessary mission into an international incident. Missions like this had the potential to end careers for anyone involved.

It probably seems a little counterintuitive that we were able to destroy city blocks with our bombs and rockets, knowing full well thousands of civilians were potentially trapped inside these towns, while at the same time preaching the importance of limited collateral damage. I thought the same thing when I first arrived, especially after reading headlines about the Ramadi campaign. But those stories lacked context. I quickly discovered there was a deliberate system in place to ensure any area we were targeting was civilian free—to the best of our knowledge, at least.

Urban warfare is messy. In general, cities are filled with infrastructure that has no military value, and there is rarely a need to destroy buildings like residences or local businesses. However, if the coalition assessed that this type of general infrastructure gained military value, it was pretty easy to get a strike approved.

This mission was a notable exception. The international community has granted extra protection to churches, mosques, schools, and similar buildings. Unless the enemy is deliberately defending them, these special types of structures are added to a no-strike list and require special permissions to destroy. The senior commander on our compound would have to personally bless off before we could strike the mosque.

In addition to infrastructure, urban environments are filled with noncombatants. These are civilians who are often only on the battlefield because that is where they live and, in this case, because ISIS wouldn't let them leave. Even if a town is actively being defended against an attacking force, many often find themselves stuck in a war they are not a part of. This aspect of urban warfare presented a unique challenge for the strike cell. If quick strikes—artillery, aircraft, or drones—were needed to support the Iraqi military's offensives, the coalition needed to be able to rapidly validate that emerging targets didn't unnecessarily risk civilian deaths. We were the good guys after all.

From my lens, initially, everything we did seemed immediate and reactive. Drones would fly and find targets across different parts of Iraq for us to destroy. However, over time I learned the process was much more deliberate. The surveillance areas weren't random, nor did drone pilots freely fly around the country. Instead, we had specific target zones we would focus on. These zones would often be activated shortly before the Iraqi military was scheduled to begin an operation, allowing us to start conducting missions in the area and soften up any defenses friendly forces would have to face. The zones would stay active for as long as we needed, but at least through to the conclusion of planned operations.

Before any area was assigned as a "target zone," it remained under extensive observation from another team. Their mission was to determine if any civilians remained in the neighborhood, identify potential ISIS strongholds, and establish sites that needed to be protected from our strikes, like a mosque or a school. Once complete, this team would present its findings to the joint task force commander for guidance and approval, with the final validation occurring at the theater level in Kuwait. I was not privy to this process and can't speak intelligently on specific assessment criteria or requirements. From my foxhole, a swath of land needed to be destroyed, and I had the perfect tool for the job.

The targeting team used the Ramadi operation as an example to explain this process to me. While successful, there were lessons to be learned and techniques that could be refined. For example, the new division reduced the size of the target zones. At the same time, the guidance from the commander was to only keep a few zones active at any given time, requiring constant updates and refinements to where he would let us off the metaphorical leash. While I wasn't in any of the decision briefs that led to this, it appeared to be an attempt to limit potential destruction overkill by providing the commander the opportunity to continually assess our progress throughout operations. By doing this, we gave him the chance to examine each new smaller target zone with a broader context that accounted for all the changing operational conditions.

Overall, this process was effective and allowed the strike cell to be reactive to the situation on the ground. Our analog and digital maps were constantly updated to reflect the status of approved and upcoming target zones. Going into a day of search and destroy, hunting for targets to strike, we knew our limitations on what we could destroy and what we needed special permission to strike. When a potential target presented itself outside the approved area, or if the destruction of a protected site became mission critical, we adjusted the process to request immediate removal of any protective status and the authority to strike.

These missions were uncommon. We didn't go around targeting schools or water-treatment facilities. But they did happen, and on this day, we would strike a mosque. But that mosque had it coming.

Our Iraqi military partners had gotten bogged down during the Hit Offensive. The fighting centered around a small mosque enemy fighters flowed in and out of and had converted into a fortified position with machine guns. We watched a few brave Iraqi service members attempt to charge this position, to be the hero of a battle nobody would remember. They failed miserably, with some paying with their lives.

After giving up trying to take the mosque themselves, the Iraqi military requested we reduce the resistance and, at a minimum, destroy the machine guns firing from the windows. The mosque didn't need to be completely destroyed. However, neutralizing it as a stronghold would undoubtedly cause substantial damage.

"All right. We're not bringing the boss over without a plan. And if we can avoid it, I don't think we turn the mosque to rubble," the director said out loud to the group. He knew the gravity of the situation. No matter what a person's faith is, a place of worship carries meaning for many people. It was a symbol, a strike that would likely be scrutinized.

The room fell silent. Everyone wanted to lead missions, but blowing up the mosque was asking for unwanted attention. "It should be me," I finally answered. "This is exactly what HIMARS is for, sir. It's our best bet," I added.

HIMARS provided an appropriate solution. The precision rockets could target specific parts of the mosque that needed to be addressed without causing extensive damage; at least when compared to the damage that would be created by dropping a 500-pound bomb.

I didn't have to fight to be selected. It was the correct answer, and nobody protested. It was my time to shine. We crafted the HIMARS aimpoints to blow out a couple of rooms the machine-gun fire appeared to be coming from, intending to destroy the weapons and kill their operators while limiting damage to the building.

"Looks good. I'll call the general's aide. What kind of damage are we talking about to the mosque? He's going to want to know," the director responded after I briefed him. He liked the plan, but we were all a little uncomfortable with what came next.

"No guarantees," I added. I was not in the business of making promises. "I should be able to take out the machine guns, and I'll do a lot less damage than a bomb would. But it's hard to tell exactly what will happen." That "should" word again; it's not a popular one to use when briefing senior leaders. But that was the best he was going to get this time. My job was to destroy things; I was brand new to the "don't quite destroy it" mentality.

While the building would gain a couple new holes in the roof, theoretically, it would survive the strike. I say theoretically because it is always hard to tell. Some of these buildings seemed ready to crumble before we arrived. Others refused to be destroyed, remaining standing with numerous holes or simply walls that wouldn't tip over even after the roof had collapsed. Again, I had zero engineering or architecture training, these are just observations from a guy who likes to make things go "boom."

The process of gaining special approval was efficient, but it was also uncomfortable. Thankfully, because the mission had to be conducted inside the strike cell, we didn't have to physically go to the monstrous operations center to brief the big boss. Instead, he came over to where we worked. He often stayed after these briefs to observe the special missions. During one of these missions later in the year, he stole my chair for the process while I was in the bathroom. It was the one strike I had to watch from the sidelines; you can't really tell the commander to get out of your seat.

But it wasn't just the big boss who came by for these uncomfortable briefs. No, he also brought his flock of colonels, the large group of senior officers I liked to avoid. Crossing paths with senior officers is always strange for me. It's like seeing the principal when you're in school or driving by a police car on the freeway. Even if you didn't do anything wrong, for some reason, it feels like you're about to be in trouble.

Before the strike cell got overcrowded with senior leaders, we conducted our standard processes for producing collateral-damage estimates, selecting the most suitable munitions, then began clearing the airspace. I provided the mission to the launchers and, once airspace was clear, I ordered them to move to the firing point.

However, based on what we had established as our standard operating procedures, I was not initially forthcoming with the target information to the launcher crews or fire-direction center at Al Asad. The last thing we needed was second guessing on our weaponeering solutions or adding another step in the process.

This is not to say I kept the targets a secret. Instead, mission details were often discussed while we waited on airspace, and we always found ourselves waiting on airspace clearance. Most of the time, I told them not to worry about it and to focus on executing their mission. In those instances, I would discuss the mission with them afterward, providing them with the official battle-damage assessments and talking through what I had observed. Sometimes, I was even able to get a recording of the strike and send it their way, allowing them to see the war the way I did.

But, for an active mission, the team at Al Asad wasn't in a deciding role. They were executors. Masters of their craft. When the strike cell approved a mission, and I gave the command to fire, there had to exist an institutional trust that what they were shooting at was legally, ethically, and morally sound. I didn't tell them we were going to fire on a place of worship that day; I don't know if I should have. They knew what was expected of them and what the responsibilities of a multiple-launch rocket system crewmember were. Just as important, they knew someone was sitting with the decision makers on their behalf, ensuring every mission was a valid target. Their job was to follow orders.

Once everything was ready, the high rollers came in for the approval brief. As I have continued in my military career since this deployment and worked for other senior leaders, I discovered that a process such as this, a formal and public-approval brief, is not a place for surprises. I'm confident this team of colonels had already been fully briefed on the situation before walking into our little hole in the wall. If any of them had an objection, it was undoubtedly addressed well before we reached this point, and the commander was tracking all of the mission details.

The commander stood between rows two and three, looking directly at the director and me, his primary advisors on either side of him. The director informed him of the situation, walking him through our decision making. However, I couldn't focus. In this solemn moment before requesting to destroy a religious sanctuary, I had a chance encounter with a friend I didn't know was a senior officer. I was in a *Charlie Brown* cartoon; all I heard was "wah-wah-wah."

In my off time, what little there was, I taught Brazilian Jiu-Jitsu to anyone on the compound who was interested. This was primarily foreign military officers and a few of the soldiers who guarded the compound. It was a very informal group. We were all on a first-name basis with no hierarchy. Well, I guess there was still some martial-arts hierarchy; the color of one's belt often means a lot in these situations. We were looking to escape our day-to-day lives and just be regular people with no titles or responsibilities for an hour a night. It turns out one of those gentlemen was the senior intelligence officer on the compound and an advisor to the general. He also didn't know where I worked. Upon recognition, he flashed a big smile that I couldn't help but match at an inappropriate time. To make matters worse, he waved. While it was probably quick and subtle, what I saw was an exaggerated *Forrest Gump* wave that would surely distract the two-star general from his brief.

At that moment, the general looked in my direction, his glare burning a hole in me. I have never met a more intense human. I was so distracted that I didn't hear the conversation. I stood there confused for a few seconds and tried to hide my grin. I quickly looked over at my friend, who nearly burst out laughing. The whole room was silent, everyone's eyes on me.

Then I realized it was my turn to brief; my role was to provide him with the technical details of the mission, without being overly technical—a unique balancing act when briefing senior leaders. I straightened up and gave my pitch. He needed to know HIMARS could do what we were selling, that my rockets could neutralize the threat and only minimally damage the mosque. Regardless of what the strike team had collectively decided, he asked for my personal and professional opinion. To him, I was "the rocket guy," the subject-matter expert on everything HIMARS.

By this point, I had done a handful of missions. While I was still earning my title, I felt confident in my knowledge of what HIMARS could do, and in my ability to leverage it in this creative way. I didn't make any promises; I have been trained to always undersell and overproduce. Probably a better motto for me than "out of sight, out of mind." To ease his concerns, I expressed my confidence in the system and the team. He approved the mission and got comfortable. This was one he was going to stay and watch. Destroying a mosque was a high-visibility mission, one he would likely have to answer questions about.

I gave the order. A few minutes later, multiple rockets impacted the mosque in quick succession, precisely where we had planned. The scene, chaos only moments prior, stood still as the smoke cleared. The building looked fine, standing proud despite the blast. Of course, there was some cosmetic damage and a couple of holes in the roof. Plus, there was likely some interior damage where the rockets detonated. But the machine guns had stopped firing, and anyone who was in the room with those machine guns was likely dead.

Shortly after, a handful of fighters fled the building. A few were gunned down by the Iraqi military, and the rest sought to set up at another location a few blocks over. I assume the majority of them were killed later that day. Most of the ISIS fighters we encountered didn't know when to just walk away and accept that they were defeated. The mission was successful; with the machine guns no longer active and the ISIS stronghold effectively abandoned, the Iraqi military was able to resume its offensive operation to liberate the town. We had achieved our tactical objective and avoided creating unnecessary damage in the process. That mission earned HIMARS some credibility with our senior leaders.

I eventually told the team back at Al Asad what they had destroyed. Like I said, it was not a secret, and they deserved to know. They just didn't need to know before they fired the rockets. That was my burden.

Is it strange that I have no qualms with that mission, even after reflection? I guess I've never viewed a building as sacred. It was a good mission, regardless of how well the collateral damage was mitigated. In fact, I would have been fine if we needed to bring the building down, destroying a mosque that was a pinnacle structure in the neighborhood for generations. There were no doubts the fighters manning those machine guns were valid military targets or that the mission saved some poor Iraqi military service member from mounting another futile charge on the fortified machine-gun position, something that had already proved a poor plan.

However, missions like this reinforced a dangerous assumption—the same one that could be drawn from Ramadi's liberation—defeating ISIS meant destroying Iraq. Sure, we could win this fight one strike at a time, but it would be at a high cost.

HIMARS would be a significant part of this destruction. At least, the system would if we could keep enough ammunition in Iraq to support the uptick in missions.

CHAPTER 13

TPS Reports

Is it weird to say that I have daddy issues? Does it sound more professional to say I have a father complex?

"When's the next resupply?" the general asked the moment he stepped into the strike cell. He announced it to the group, letting the question linger, but it was directed at me. It wasn't the first time he had asked. It wasn't even the first time that day. It wouldn't be the last. Our logistics were struggling to keep pace with the increase in ammunition expenditure. Rockets were in the fight, which caught many people outside of Iraq off guard.

It shouldn't have.

"Still finalizing the details, sir. I'll reach out again and see if I can get some clarity," I replied. I knew it was not the answer he wanted. But it was better than saying, "I don't know."

"Get it done, I'm not letting us go black on rockets, Brennan," he said. He was stern but didn't raise his voice. He was frustrated, and for good reason. We were running out of rockets. Fast. Our support elements had disregarded our assessments and were now scrambling to play catch up.

HIMARS had become a hot commodity in my first two months in Iraq. I warned anyone who would listen that my rockets were about to become a critical asset. But who was I? I could scream into the wind; nobody was listening to a random Army captain. Especially one who clearly wanted to fire more rockets. Instead, people with more rank continually provided data on historical rocket expenditures as a rebuttal to my warnings. This was a silly metric that discounted the situation we were facing and failed to account for the fact the historical data they were quick to cite did not include an offensive operation so close to the HIMARS firing point.

"Until further notice, HIMARS are for emergencies only, my approval for any release," the general said to our director. Then he looked back at me, "I need you in the fight, kid. Get me more rockets. And do it fast. I want an actual assessment by the end of the day, no more bullshit updates."

I wanted to fix the issue. I had finally proved the system's worth, and rocket artillery had become a staple of our strike-warfare strategy. I was in the fight and was not ready to go back to sitting on the sidelines in my little corner, ignored.

At the same time, I didn't want to let the general down. I would be crushed if he ever told me he was disappointed in me.

I didn't have positive male role models growing up. My parents divorced when I was nine, and my older brother left around the same time. They would be out of my life for years. I grew up fast and always found myself being the old man in my circle of friends, the responsible one.

Sports coaches often filled the gap left behind after I stopped all communication with my father—a fickle relationship since reaching adulthood. But these relationships were always fleeting, seasonal by nature. The military hierarchal structure filled this need. I latched on to commanders and other senior leaders in search of mentorship.

Some of these men were great people of character and embraced the role. They weren't simply bosses. Instead, I looked to them more as father figures or older brothers, replacing relationships lost in my youth. I sometimes wonder if they ever knew how meaningful these relationships were to me personally and professionally. Of course, I would never tell them. That's how we operate; too proud to be vulnerable. I had hoped the general I served with in Iraq would read this and know he was an important role model, that he made an important impact on me as an Army officer and a man. Sadly, he died while I was writing this memoir.

Other men were weak, selfish, or just not people I could respect. I worked with both types in Iraq. I was taken under the wing of a strong noncommissioned officer, accepted as a member of a team, and trusted by a senior leader. At the same time, I was belittled, censored, and had my career threatened over trivial issues. When I was in the strike cell, I was in leadership limbo. It was unclear who I worked for, and people were quick to capitalize on the situation. This created a weird balance, one complicated by my battalion commander, a man I didn't respect. It was a situation that nearly drove me out of the service.

Ambiguity in the exact structure of the chain of command presents a unique challenge for liaison officers. At times, it's not clear who you work for and what level of authority different people have over you. This hierarchical gray area is relatively easy to navigate for those looking to avoid work. However, the muddy relationship can become quite burdensome during constant operations, particularly when the liaison becomes the linchpin to success. This is especially true in a military setting, where many officers define themselves by their power over others and often confuse their rank with authority. This situation was tough to work through, and I found myself on the losing end of many problems as an easy scapegoat, the most important of which was just getting more ammunition, a prerequisite to doing my job and a requirement for supporting Iraqi operations in central Iraq.

It didn't take me long to deduce the heart of the problem: everyone assumed they were my boss.

My first set of bosses were those at Union III, our small compound in Baghdad. While I would like to think I worked for one or two people on the base, a handful of others probably felt different, particularly those who outranked me. This created confusion between the people asking me for help and those ordering me to do something; these are two very different things. Everything I did was to enable the strike cell's missions. However, my role was also clearly defined. I worked as the HIMARS subject-matter expert, preparing briefs for senior leadership, developing target packets, and prosecuting fire missions. While I pride myself on being a team player, it can't be at the expense of my actual responsibilities. So, if someone asked me for help with a project, I would help as best I could. At the same time, I was not just another body for busy work.

This created a big divide in the strike cell at one point as one of the directors, a major, misinterpreted his authority over all the liaison teams, embracing the role as if he was a senior commander and we were his staff. This relationship eventually hit a boiling point. When challenged, the director worked to solve the problem by removing people from the group. When he threatened to throw me out, I smiled and told him he could find me at the gym, then wished him luck in prosecuting any future HIMARS missions. This was probably not the most professional response, but it felt good at the time.

Senior leaders on Union III eventually reined him in. However, this was a wake-up call for me. It highlighted the importance of defining relationships and the fact that different leadership styles were required to manage people I didn't have direct authority over.

My second boss was in Kuwait, a major. Our battalion executive officer—who was eventually replaced by our operations officer—served as the officer in charge of our HIMARS unit forward. While I often wished this was where I received my guidance and support—as this was where my evaluation originated—these leaders simply provided mentorship and a place to vent. And vent I did. It was nice to have a support chain, but at the same time, they couldn't help me. I was on my own. They were hundreds of miles away and had no influence over operations in Iraq.

My third boss, the lieutenant colonel battalion commander, remained back in the United States. We didn't talk much, if at all. My mission was not his concern, and I was not interested in what he had to say. If you can't tell from reading this, we didn't get along. However, whether I liked it or not, this was my actual boss at the end of the day. While this should have been my most straightforward relationship, it was probably the most challenging. Our personalities clashed, forcing information to generally be passed between us secondhand. This strained relationship made my job much more complex than it needed to be.

My final bosses were from a field-artillery brigade stationed in Jordan. They provided oversight of artillery in the Middle East. However, Iraq was outside their jurisdiction. Because of this, they were generally an out-of-sight, out-of-mind problem. To be honest, I didn't know they tracked me at all until they threatened to investigate me over a mission they deemed an excessive expenditure of ammunition.

The strike in question was actually quite simple. The building was no different than any of the others we had previously destroyed, a near-perfect square a little bigger than most. However, it was a high-visibility target, drawing extra scrutiny. At least a dozen people, including some ISIS leadership, were inside the building. This mission was critical for shaping a neighborhood in preparation for an upcoming Iraqi military offensive. In turn, the general took notice, and I did not want to disappoint him.

The targeting officer and I built a standard weaponeering solution, proposing we destroy the building with four HIMARS rockets, each one near a corner of the building. We were fairly confident the building would collapse. Again, I must point out we had zero architectural knowledge and the Army had not had the foresight to equip our cell with a structural engineer or demolitions expert. Still, because of its size, we couldn't be sure all the rooms would be blown out. Even if the mission was successful, there was no guarantee we would kill everyone inside.

The general looked at us and sternly said, "No one leaves that building alive." Understanding his guidance, we reworked the mission, increasing the proposal to six rockets. "Better," was all he said. But the stern face transitioned to a big grin when the rockets started impacting. Four might have been enough; it's hard to tell. Six rockets left no doubt. The building was rubble, and no one walked out.

Less than 24 hours later, I received an e-mail demanding I justify our weaponeering solution, accusing us of wasting "precious ammunition." It was an easy conversation once the general said he supported the decision. Still, it let me know other people were watching, and they had a presumed level of authority over me.

These relationship challenges culminated in one silly event that nearly ended my career. The drama wasn't because a mission went astray or civilians were killed, but because someone's feelings were hurt in an e-mail. After all, this was war.

Once the Hit Offensive began, ammunition expenditures were off the charts, straining the untested logistics system. At the same time, there was a demand for more firing locations. While the range of the platform is impressive, it couldn't cover the whole country. Plans were developed to establish HIMARS positions to support border missions near Syria and the upcoming Mosul fight. This meant the field-artillery brigade that provided HIMARS support had to balance the requirements of supplying ammunition for current operations with staging ammunition for future ones.

We found ourselves nearly out of ammunition after three days of record-level HIMARS missions supporting the Iraqi offensive. The strike-cell leadership, including the general, was not pleased. While I had warned people for at least two weeks that our rocket expenditures would be very high, the ammunition consumption flabbergasted all the support elements outside of Iraq. When I checked on the next delivery, as directed, I discovered the next batch was headed for prepositioning, not to resupply us in central Iraq.

This was a serious problem I needed to address right away or find myself out of the fight, and potentially on the wrong end of an ass chewing for failing to accomplish such a simple task.

I started with my first set of bosses on Union III. The leadership on my compound confirmed the site pending delivery didn't need ammunition for another few weeks at the earliest, likely not for another month or two.

We had made a mistake.

I reached out to my second set of bosses for some guidance. However, all I received was some moral support. While this was appreciated, it wasn't helpful. The supporting element needed to adjust the subsequent delivery, which had to be fixed immediately to be changed in time for shipment. We were almost out of the fight because we lacked ammunition, so I acted, contacting my third set of bosses, the random artillery unit in Jordan.

I reached out at the action-officer level, which is supposed to be a safe space and the venue for handling issues without involving decision makers. I sent an e-mail that identified the problem, relayed the guidance I had received from the leadership at Union III, and recommended a simple solution.

We got the rockets but accidentally kicked the proverbial hornets' nest by refusing to allow the status quo. I became the squeaky wheel, so to speak. And that came with consequences.

The main building at the firing point at Al Asad Air Base, Iraq, where soldiers spent their time when not conducting missions. February 2016.

Most places that housed the US military had a bunker like this one at Al Asad, seen in July 2016, or other designated-cover areas to increase survivability against incoming enemy rockets and mortars, the biggest threat in this type of war.

HIMARS launchers wait in hiding until called for a mission. Ironically, these types of covered areas in central Iraq became common HIMARS targets. Photo taken at Al Asad in September 2016.

A HIMARS launcher rolls off an aircraft in a HIMARS rapid infiltration exercise, also known as a HIRAIN, at Fort Lewis, Washington, in the summer of 2018. The ability to load HIMARS launchers onto aircraft and have the firing team able to roll off ready to begin mission processing makes the systems a uniquely valuable indirect-fire tool. (Kara Dasalla)

A HIMARS crew chief races his launcher to the firing point after receiving the command from the strike cell. Photo taken in July 2016.

HIMARS crews qualifying on their launchers in early 2016 by firing the reduced-range practice rocket in Kuwait before moving to the firing point in Iraq.

August 2016 and both Al Asad HIMARS launchers are aimed at a target awaiting the command to fire.

By having both the HIMARS launchers fire together at the same target, we could increase the destructive effects and limit enemy reactions. It was the third rocket I was always concerned about; the few seconds between the first impacts and the follow-up rockets provided a small window for enemy fighters to flee. Photo taken at Al Asad in June 2016.

A single precision rocket erupts from a HIMARS launcher at Al Asad in August 2016, beginning its path toward an ISIS stronghold.

There was a limit to how much extra ammunition we could store at the firing point as it not only took up a lot of space, as shown in this August 2016 image, but each pod is essentially a bomb.

A HIMARS resupply vehicle prepares to move ammunition in August 2016. Because of the sheer weight of the pods, a crane is needed to conduct the resupply, which is expected to take around twenty minutes.

It was not uncommon for us to have a loadout like the one depicted here in July 2016, with one launcher nearly empty and the other full or almost full. This picture also highlights the corrosive residue left behind after missions that can damage the launcher if not cleaned regularly.

An indelible trail of smoke remains as the rockets cut their path through the sky. In an environment as open as Iraq, it was not difficult for enemy forces to find our firebases. Luckily for us, ISIS rarely took the fight to the Americans forward deployed in Iraq. Photo taken in July 2016.

Both HIMARS launchers firing an October 2016 mission together from Al Asad, enabling multiple near-simultaneous impacts against the target.

Twin fireballs illuminate the night sky as HIMARS rockets remind the enemy that strike cell operations never rest. Photo taken in the summer of 2016.

An up-close view of a guided rocket breaking through the pod cover during its launch from Al Asad in October 2016. These breakaway covers are fabricated to split, protecting the rocket when stored but not hindering the munition during its launch. After the missions, the covers become a hot commodity because they can be easily turned into a plaque that can be presented to senior leaders, distinguished visitors, or as going-away gifts for rocket-artillery soldiers.

Although the rockets themselves were designed to minimize collateral damage, the sheer force required to shoot a 200-pound projectile over fifty kilometers creates quite the controlled explosion. Photo taken in the summer of 2016.

It turns out many people suffer from imposter syndrome, doubting themselves and questioning their competence. When someone makes waves, questions a decision, or highlights a potential mistake, it can crack the confident facade on display. Once this happens, the reaction is unpredictable. In this case, they attacked the messenger, which happened to be me.

I spent the next few hours on the phone with majors, scrambling to defend the tone of my e-mail. I was shocked at how emotional people were, but I found most of the reprimand pretty comical. At the end of the day, I didn't work for these people. Earlier in life, I had failed miserably as a mixed martial artist. Having the experience of receiving a brutal beating in a cage in front of my friends and family made a little yelling not that bothersome. So, I took the tongue lashing and let some officers vent their frustrations, a likely buildup from numerous deployment issues. Still, I had learned another lesson. Sadly, ignoring a problem and hoping someone else raises the red flag is often the better, or at least safer, career decision. I also learned the messenger is an easy target; a position to avoid.

The most embarrassing part of this ordeal was they called my battalion commander back in the United States. It was like they were telling on me. In the Army, the joke is that someone filed a "Hurt Feelings Report." My commander was furious, and I'm confident this single exchange shaped the mediocre evaluation that eventually followed a few months later. I couldn't know for sure, though, because when I asked to sit down to talk with him, he refused.

I didn't care much about what this man thought. He had no business being the commander; the Army does not always get it right. However, he said something that day that stuck with me, shifted my paradigm, and made me reconsider my mission.

He asked if I understood my purpose as the HIMARS liaison and if I knew why I was in Iraq. I confidently explained my role in supporting the Iraqi military, liberating towns, destroying ISIS, and developing techniques for employing rocket artillery in combat. Not in his eyes. For him, I was there to build partnerships with other coalition forces, network for our unit, and schmooze with some senior leaders. The war was just a venue, the backdrop for our unit to gain some prestige.

This was a hard realization for me. For many, the Iraqi military and its mission didn't matter. The Iraqis were not our allies, and their success was insignificant in the grand scheme. In my boss' eyes, being effective with HIMARS only mattered if it made our unit look good. The number of ISIS fighters or Iraqi military members who died in this awful country was unimportant.

While I disagreed, was the way I tracked my missions in an Excel spreadsheet much different from this sentiment? I selfishly wanted to succeed; this simply meant increasing my statistics. Realistically, I couldn't care less about the actual operations. I didn't care about the towns of Hit or Kubaysah. I wouldn't lose any sleep if we leveled Fallujah and the historic town became unlivable ruins. In fact, outside of the days when there was a chance for me to get in the fight, I hardly even stayed abreast of what the Iraqi military was doing. This became especially true once the mission transitioned outside my HIMARS range ring. Instead, my focus was internal. I planned to set records for the number of rockets fired and kill as many ISIS fighters as possible. At the end of the day, it became a numbers game for me.

CHAPTER 14

A Numbers Game

Sadly, the most important bullet in recent wars has often been the one written on officer-evaluation reports.

Army leaders are trained to quantify everything they do. This data serves as supporting evidence for qualitative assessments, with statistics becoming the foundation of evaluations and awards. This lesson of tracking and compiling even the most insignificant accomplishments was ingrained in me as a cadet in the Reserve Officer Training Corps and is something I have carried with me throughout my career. The statistics and experiences unique to combat zones are a way to build up an Army resume, a necessity to stand out in a sea of talented officers. On my first deployment, I tracked the number of patrols I conducted, the prisoners we processed, the dollar value of equipment I was responsible for, and my team's fitness metrics, something the Army is weirdly obsessed with. Tracking this type of data was, and is, the norm. Anyone who says otherwise is lying.

A few days after I arrived in Iraq in 2016, I saw the ultimate statistics sheet, a collection of numbers that epitomized a successful strike-cell deployment. One of the strike directors, who was deployed as an individual augmentee, left just as I assumed my position in the strike cell. He had served in the position for months, overseeing the infamous Ramadi campaign. The general presented him with his deployment award, with the accompanying narrative proclaiming his accomplishments as the strike director. His tour had included hundreds of missions, countless buildings destroyed, and an incredible number of enemies killed.

It was an impressive list of combat statistics, an awe-inspiring moment for me as the new guy. I was envious. I was anxious. I quickly became determined to build similar resume bullets, to start racking up statistics and doing my share of the killing.

I remember the director's farewell speech well. His words stuck with me then and have stayed with me for years, a strange reminder to not miss the forest for the trees. He was proud of what had been accomplished during his time in Iraq and what the strike cell had done as a collective organization under his leadership. At the same time, he expressed reservations about our mission, struggling to find meaning beyond each strike. What had been the point of his efforts? He said he didn't know our purpose in Iraq or if we had accomplished anything through our actions, that the country's future remained uncertain but the outlook was grim. By all accounts, Iraq was a failed state and our efforts were only making the problem worse.

His reflection ended abruptly, but his musings would linger. Then, to fill the awkward silence that followed his somber reflection, he said, "but we sure killed a bunch of those bastards." That we did.

We all laughed. This was what the mission had become. We didn't know what the Iraqi military would accomplish or the level of commitment the United States was willing to take for a mission it had already deemed complete. Instead, each person focused on their individual mission without much sense of the greater purpose beyond the broad "defeat the enemy" mantra that can be applied to every war. Success became an individual endeavor. Each person had to ask themselves what they had done on the deployment, ignoring all the surrounding context and politics. For me, that meant a tracker.

I didn't know what needed to be tracked, so I started with everything. I created columns in an Excel spreadsheet for missions conducted, enemy killed, enemy wounded, buildings destroyed, vehicles destroyed, and indirect-fire systems destroyed. If you could shoot it, I had a column for it. Better to have all the data upfront and distill it down later. I quickly started filling in columns: two missions here, four rockets there, a building destroyed with five people inside, etc.

It grew. I was insatiable. Every short-term goal achieved just led to more goals. Could I get 100 of these or 200 of that? It was unclear what was realistic for longer-term goals, however. The war could end any day, at least our part of it, anyway. So, I took it one mission at a time, fighting for every opportunity to be involved.

I was not alone in this endeavor. The Air Force team tracked similar statistics. Interestingly, they measured their munitions column in tonnage dropped instead of the number of bombs. We bragged to each other, one-upping the other when we could. It was a game, and it fueled our competition. These statistics should not have meant so much to me. But they did. For a short period of my life, these numbers were everything. It's funny that what drove me every day then, what I thought would define my military career, is now meaningless.

Still, at the time, I ensured my evaluations and awards were overflowing with data regarding fire missions; death was the ultimate measurement of my success. The pursuit of these numbers never skewed a weaponeering solution. Instead, it made us compete to be the agent of destruction, even if we were not always the asset best suited for the mission.

I don't regret battle tracking. Communicating my platform's contributions to the war effort was beneficial to more than just me. I'm not ashamed that I developed a spreadsheet to tally my kill count. I understood my mission; these statistics were the measures of performance and effectiveness for my entire battalion and, arguably, rocket artillery as a viable tool in modern war. These numbers fed the Army narrative regarding the modernization of long-range precision fires. However, the desire to excel in this context led me down a dark path toward a mission I will never forget and an action I will not forgive myself for.

"Sir, we got a report of mortar tracks just outside Kubaysah, not sure on casualties," the battle captain announced. "We should have visual of the POO site in just a minute." You read that right. POO site, pronounced just like it's spelled. It stands for the point of origin, the spot where the enemy launches a mortar, rocket, or fires a round of artillery from a cannon. Our acronyms are out of control. I can only imagine the conversations that led to this one. POO, what were they thinking?

Friendly radar assets had identified an enemy mortar firing position in our area. The drone didn't take long to get overhead and assess the suspected location.

"That's definitely a mortar site," the director commented. "I count at least seven or eight dismounts." There was a single mortar tube and a handful of enemy fighters moving around the area. In our lingo, the term dismount is used to distinguish the fighters who are walking, like light infantry, from enemy forces in vehicles. This is not generally a necessary distinction in a conflict like the one we were fighting, but it is ingrained into us while we conduct large pretend wars—exercises—against mechanized military forces.

"Official word is ten, sir, drone team just dropped it in the chat," someone added after seeing the update. "Looks like they are pretty spread out and using that little shack to store ammunition." The enemy fighters had positioned the mortar tube approximately twenty-five meters from a medium-sized shack. We watched them moving mortar rounds from the shack to the mortar tube, potentially preparing for a fire mission.

"Any idea on who they are targeting?" the director asked.

"They're too far away from Al Asad to hit our guys," the battle captain responded. "I'll check next door and get an update on the Iraqi positions in the area."

"Smart. But I doubt they have accurate data, you know how the Iraqis are," the director added. "Either way, I don't want another mortar leaving that tube. If they load a round, I want a Hellfire smashing into the position before they can fire."

"Roger, sir, standing by with Hellfire," the drone liaison acknowledged.

The director put out his guidance for the mission: "The way I see it, we have three targets. We have the ammunition shack, the mortar tube, and the enemy fighters. I'd like to hit all three together, if possible, I don't want them to scatter at the first sign of trouble."

"Rockets are the best bet for a simultaneous strike," I chimed in. I made sure to propose a solution first, not allowing my Air Force counterpart to beat me to the punch. "I can do three rockets. The first two will land at the same time, the third just a few seconds after. We'll use a point-detonation fuze for the tube itself. It won't completely destroy it, but I doubt anyone will ever fire from it again. At the same, we could use a delay fuze on that little shack, hopefully getting some secondary explosions. During the chaos those big booms create, I'll explode a rocket above the stragglers and rain some death shrapnel down on any of the runners." Some heads perked up at the term "death shrapnel," it piqued a lot of people's interest, including the director.

Rocket artillery was a good solution and I sold it well. Three targets, three aim points, with a focus on the desired effects for each one and synchronized in order to maximize lethality. This was an easy mission to rack up some statistics on my tracker for rockets fired and enemies killed. Having come into my own, I considered it an elegant solution. I also wanted to see the proximity fuze in action; I needed to understand all facets of the weapon system.

"I like it. Do it! Sorry, ALO, it was a good pitch," the director replied. The air-liaison officer didn't have a chance to get a word in. "Besides, I want to see this 'death shrapnel' from the air burst." The director loved the plan as much as he loved my confidence. I received the authorization to prosecute the mission and quickly worked out the details on my artillery computer.

I was excited to finally observe the proximity fuze in action. Although plenty of our missions had targeted troops in the open, this was the first time I was the lead; it was the first time rockets would be fired into a crowd. It wouldn't be the last. This was inherently different than blowing up a building full of people, knowing bodies were under the rubble. No, with the proximity fuze, there would be no assuming success; we would have front-row seats to an execution, and I would be the executioner.

We cleared the airspace surprisingly quickly. I moved the launchers to the firing point and received final engagement approval. "Shot! ... All rockets fired."

We watched the people at the mortar site casually conducting operations, going about their business, unaware death was racing toward them. It was a strange feeling. About ninety seconds later, we saw rockets drop from the sky a split second before impact. The first two impacted at the same time. The ammunition shack explosion was massive, scattering debris in every direction, including into enemy fighters. The mortar-tube explosion, while dramatically smaller, was equally as satisfying. There was no doubt everyone working near the tube was dead, and I would be shocked if the mortar tube was ever usable again.

The next few seconds felt like an eternity. "Don't move! Don't you fucking move!" I yelled it at the top of my lungs, urging the last couple of stragglers to stay where they were. I felt the director's eyes on me, displeased with the outburst and frustrated with my potty mouth. But I didn't care; those were future problems. This moment was mine, and I knew he wouldn't interrupt my mission for his weird aversion to curse words.

I expected anyone not directly hit by the first two rockets to flee, running in any direction so long as it was far from where they had just witnessed the might of HIMARS. I expected chaos. While one or two had the survival instincts to escape the horror scene, others froze. Dumbfounded. How long would they have stood there, unable to act? After only a few heartbeats, the final rocket appeared.

This was a new experience. I'm not sure what I wanted to see, but it was not visually impressive. The rocket burst well above the ground; a puff of smoke was all we saw. I didn't see the shrapnel. While we created an ominous cloud above the remaining fighters, we couldn't see the infamous steel rain. That is not to say, however, that it wasn't there. Although there may not have been a fireworks display, the munition worked exactly as it was supposed to. It was highly effective; no fighters remained standing.

It was a perfect mission. Sure, a couple scampered away in the chaos, but the weaponeering was flawless. There was hardly any evidence the mortar position or the ammunition shack had ever existed outside a handful of debris and a tube on its side. I counted seven bodies. I was so proud. I felt like an artist, continually improving my methods as I gained more experience with my tools and learned the nuance of my canvas.

The official battle-damage assessment posted: "Mortar tube destroyed, weapons cache destroyed, six enemies killed, one enemy wounded."

Wounded? I couldn't believe it.

"Bullshit!" I yelled at the monitor, once again drawing the director's attention. This time, with the mission complete, I couldn't ignore his glare. "Sir, nobody's surviving that, at least not for long. He'll be dead in a few minutes, and everyone knows it," I said, preempting the awkward conversation about professionalism I knew was coming.

Sometimes, people refuse to die. I was often impressed by this resilience. When someone crawls out of rubble or climbs out of a burning car, they earn another shot at life. But I always assume their death is near, either from internal bleeding or the next inevitable strike. As frustrated as we would be, you can't take that determination away from survivors. Those stats are what they are.

That was not the case this day. Nobody hobbled away from this battleground in search of safety. If anyone was still alive, they wouldn't be for long.

Overall, the mission was great, and the team was ready to move on, my complaint notwithstanding. Despite my protest, the drone feed transitioned to another area in search of our next target. But we had nothing else pressing, no emergency to respond to. Instead, we began hunting to see if we could find someone else to kill. When we weren't directly supporting an Iraqi offensive, this is what we did. We hunted the approved target areas in an attempt to win the war one strike at a time.

I should have accepted the success of the strike and appreciated the statistics; it was a good mission. I should have moved on. Better yet, I should have taken a moment to reflect on the gravity of the mission, on the lives I had just taken. "Should" is all well and good, but I did none of those things. I was insatiable.

After a few minutes of searching, it was clear we wouldn't find a new target anytime soon. So, I requested an updated assessment of the mortar firing point. I refused to accept a "wounded" in my spreadsheet if I didn't have to. A good mission didn't wound people, it killed them. My request was approved, and the drone was repurposed for an updated battle-damage assessment.

As the drone reassessed the scene, we watched on our central, top-row television. Finding the survivor didn't take long; it was clear he wouldn't last. The pilot sent me a message on my laptop: "No change."

Still, it was hard to give up on the mission, knowing the wounded fighter was on death's doorstep. He was writhing around in the field, obviously in immense pain but unable to do much more than shift from side to side. From our angle, it looked like one of his legs was blown off. He was likely also bleeding internally from the blast and his body shredded from shrapnel. Without immediate medical care, he would be dead any minute. No one was coming. We knew it. He knew it. He was dead already and was just waiting for the end. The pilot asked me for permission to move on and to allow him to resume his search for another target.

I'm not proud of what happened next.

"Request denied." I sent the message without much consideration.

Selfishly, I wanted to get the credit I thought I deserved for the mission. It was excellently designed and I felt like I was being snubbed. I felt cheated. I needed that one additional kill to add to the tracker. I craved that measure of effectiveness.

So, I continued to watch the feed. Worse, I forced everyone else to watch. I don't know how many people watched that feed as it live streamed in the strike cell and who knows where else. Not to mention the recorded version that was likely heavily distributed, as it was a pretty neat mission. At a minimum, this included the drone pilot and anyone on his team, but I'm not sure where they operated, as well as everyone in the strike cell. Whether they wanted to watch or not, we kept one screen focused on this defeated fighter as he bled out.

He was alone. He was forgotten. It didn't take long for him to die. Given the excitement of the mission, and the fact our videos had no sound, his passing was rather anti-climactic. He finally just stopped moving.

"Battle damage update: seven enemy killed," I read it out loud for the team, dramatically louder than necessary and a little bit smug, proud of the extra statistics. A victory. However, it was like winning an argument at the cost of a friendship. I was so wrapped up in my statistics that I lost sight of what I was doing; I lost track of who I was. I look back and am disgusted at how unsympathetic I was, at how little I cared about this horror.

One of my friends from the second row turned around, disappointed: "Dark, bro." Then he went right back to work.

We never talked about that day, and nobody brought it up later, not even to joke about. A mission to be forgotten, if possible. It didn't bother me at the time. In fact, the opposite. In my mind, my friend was a whiner who needed to "soldier up." This was what we had signed up for. That man was dead either way. Choosing to watch him die didn't change his fate. It didn't create undue suffering.

Still, it was unnecessary.

I have forgotten many things from my time in Iraq, but three or four missions will always stay with me. Watching that man squirm and writhe in the field and eventually die alone is one of those memories. Sadly, I'm the reason a handful of my peers were forced to share that experience; why that drone pilot and his team had to watch. I'm the reason why many other service members will also hold onto that memory.

I'm okay with the mission; those men needed to die. But forcing everyone around me to watch one man's suffering is something I don't forgive myself for. It crossed a line. However, at the time, I didn't care. I was happy to be doing my part. I didn't think about how these experiences would affect any of us. I didn't think about how that moment would impact me in reflection.

But please don't forget this was ISIS we were killing. The bad guys. Don't feel sympathy for these men; they made their bed and needed to be stopped. This was a necessity. There would be no reasoning with ISIS.

It's worth noting, however, that I felt justified in killing ISIS because they were evil, not because Iraq was worth saving. The rest of the Iraqi people were not good, and they were not, and still are not, our friends. Sadly, the longer I supported the Iraqi military, the more I realized this fact. I started to see the same problems I observed in 2011. I distrusted them and wondered why they were not left to fight this war alone. Part of me wished we would leave them to their own devices, even if that meant they would fail.

CHAPTER 15

To Their Own Devices

We spoiled them rotten; why were we surprised by their incompetence?

My previous deployment had soured my opinion of the Iraqi military, highlighting defects that couldn't simply be written off as aspects of their culture. In 2011, I witnessed Iraqi officers treat their enlisted counterparts as servants, physically abuse prisoners, and demonstrate toxic greed and corruption. Because I didn't work with them directly when fighting ISIS, the only Iraqi forces I had to deal with were the ones on my television. Out of sight, out of mind. Initially, I didn't associate these warfighters with the corrupt Iraqi military I had served with five years prior. However, once operations intensified, my disdain for these people returned.

It needs to be stated up front that while my comments may disparage the Iraqi military as an institution, at the individual level there were undoubtedly brave soldiers and great leaders who fought against ISIS. All militaries are filled with heroes who sacrificed everything to save their country or were willing to lay down their lives for their brothers in arms. The Iraqi military is no exception. There were hard-fought battles to liberate Iraqi cities from the ruthless extremists. Urban warfare required close-quarters combat, and the destructive tools leveraged by the coalition turned these cities into brutal war zones. While the West may have dominated the battlefield with our technology, credit must be given to the Iraqi military members who courageously stood up to ISIS, many knowing their lives may be forfeited.

However, while it's easy to craft this successful narrative and focus on the positives in retrospection, at the time there was frustration among those of us who directly supported Iraqi operations. It didn't take long for me to echo the sentiment of the random officer at my first targeting meeting and openly start asking why we continued to support the Iraqi military. We made them reliant on our technology, incapable of conducting operations without significant technological overmatch. The massive Iraqi military force was halted at every obstacle, some as simple as a single gunman firing from a window. They would wait, expectant that the strike cell would fix their problems. They knew our success was dependent on their success. So, like a parent giving in to a spoiled child, we gave them whatever they asked for.

We couldn't sustain this operational approach, though. It's not feasible or prudent to systematically destroy every building an enemy fighter decides to defend. We were signing ourselves up to protect these people and continue to fight their battles. From the tactical point of view, for the soldiers liberating these towns, this approach reduced the unit's risk of receiving casualties, even if it was at the cost of destroying their country. It's hard to blame a commander for not needlessly throwing his soldiers' lives away. But it was more than risk aversion and timidity that pushed me over the edge and reminded me of who the Iraqis really were. Instead, it was gross incompetence and collusion with the enemy.

The Iraqis' allegiance was always in question. They were not our friends. They were partners of circumstance, tools to a strategic end. Sometimes I would forget that. By sheer proximity, most people build some sort of relationship with those they work with, but I never felt comfortable putting my life in their hands, something I avoided whenever possible. In my experience, these relationships had to be closely monitored and controlled as they left us vulnerable.

For example, in 2011, Iraqis on the compound I lived on regularly alerted insurgents of our movement and often compromised our patrols. To counter this, we communicated our mission specifics with the least number of people possible and sometimes even confiscated people's phones.

On my first deployment, we struggled to trust our interpreters, military partners, or Iraqi civilian leadership. Even when training the Iraqi military was our primary mission, we remained wary of our partners. When conducting rifle-marksmanship training with Iraqi soldiers, we were required to have a US soldier man a machine gun pointed at the trainees. Why, you ask? Because, in 2010, an Afghan soldier stood up, turned around, and proceeded to kill his US counterparts. Then it happened again, and again, and again. Dozens of these so-called "insider attacks" plagued the coalition effort in both Iraq and Afghanistan. They amounted to one thing: trust problems. In 2011, many Iraqis worked with Iranian terrorists who were happy to see Iraq burn if it meant the United States struggled. Why would supporting ISIS be any different?

Trust in the Iraqis couldn't exist for most of us who had previously served with the Iraqi military. During Operation *Inherent Resolve*, the Iraqis were not privy to our intelligence, and we didn't divulge much about our strike operations. This was a combination of classification restrictions and operational security. We didn't trust them. However, we were supporting them at the end of the day and had to occasionally share information.

While the fact that we worked with the Iraqis was something I was able to keep out of my mind, for others, this was the focus of their deployment. Many of the senior leaders on my compound had Iraqi counterparts. During the offensives to regain lost territory, this often meant a lot of cross-communication. Sometimes we would receive strike requests from senior Iraqi officers on the compound, like our mosque strike, relayed through a senior US officer. Other times, some senior leaders would feel obligated to provide an Iraqi general officer with situational awareness about an upcoming strike. During one of these engagements, I was reminded of the rampant corruption in the Iraqi military.

One afternoon, we identified a group of ISIS fighters congregating outside, just a few miles from the Iraqi military conducting offensive operations. Our partners had halted again, relying on our armed drones to root out any direct resistance before continuing. The ISIS group we identified didn't look like they were leaving anytime soon, so we decided to interrupt their meeting with a single HIMARS rocket. Because of the surrounding buildings, I selected a point-detonation fuze instead of the preferred method of raining shrapnel down from above. I wasn't sure exactly what this type of explosion would do to a human body. But if we came anywhere close to a direct hit with a fuze designed for destroying vehicles, these enemy fighters were going to be blown to pieces. We were all a little curious to see the results. The general approved the strike, but we again found ourselves waiting on some last-minute airspace issues.

The US Army colonel who often served as our link to the Iraqi operations center took the mission information next door. While this was not the norm, it occasionally happened, particularly when strikes could interfere with Iraqi operations. The last thing we needed was the friendly troops on the ground assuming ISIS had just detonated some sort of improvised explosive device. Such an assumption would likely halt operations for an extended period. Shortly after the colonel walked into the Iraqi operations center, our airspace manager announced we were clear. I ordered my team to fire, and we played the waiting game as the rockets flew toward the group of enemy fighters.

"They're not going to stand around waiting forever, Brennan," the director said while staring at the drone. He was regularly frustrated with how long it took from launch to impact; we all were. "How long?"

"Just under two minutes, sir. Doesn't look like they're going anywhere," I replied. "It'll be worth the wait." I was excited about the upcoming carnage. We all were. A good strike really broke up the monotony of a slow day.

We watched intently. A lot can happen in two minutes. In fact, the situation on the ground often changed slightly while our rockets flew. However, until this day, those changes were all random circumstances, a hint of luck to leave at the last minute or the fatal decision to enter a building right before an explosion. But this time was different; this time my mission was sabotaged.

We watched the group standing in their little huddle, unaware death was racing toward them. The video quality from our drones was surprisingly good. While we couldn't necessarily distinguish between two different individuals' facial features, identifying their actions was simple.

"Did that dude just answer his phone?" someone blurted from the front. "I wonder if he knows that will be his last call. Can you imagine being on the other line when the rocket hits?" We all laughed. But this was a call he would be glad he took.

While there was no sound, the context was clear from his body language; something was wrong. We watched, piecing it together with the body language of the fighter on the phone. The laughter stopped as we realized what was happening. Then, suddenly, numerous people looked up at the sky.

"We got a leak! Someone is fucking calling him!" I yelled. I was furious.

Barely a ten-second call, and the group scattered in every direction, a mad dash for survival. Our teammates had compromised our mission. Someone from the Iraqi operations center had used our mission information to call and warn this group about the imminent strike. One of the Iraqi military officers on Union III was doing everything in their power to protect ISIS, or maybe just this one small group. Maybe his brother or best friend was among them. Honestly, I didn't care how he justified his treasonous actions. He had colluded with the enemy. Worse, he ruined my mission and made me waste a rocket.

The rocket hit less than a minute later, but no one was around. The mission failed, and those men likely melted back into the ranks of defenders. I like to think their luck changed shortly after that, that they found a safe building to hunker down in, only to be victims in another strike later that day. Based on how the war continued to progress, I doubt anyone in that group is still alive.

But the traitor probably is. He has probably continued to climb the ranks, willing to do whatever is needed, even at the cost of his nation's survival.

How many times was there a phone call like this one? Some panicked officer providing a warning to his friends at the hint of a potential strike on their position or divulging Iraqi military plans. Most of the time, these treasonous actions probably didn't amount to anything. But on this day, it saved some lives, although probably only temporarily.

There was no investigation or accusations. Everyone knew what had happened, but we had to save face. Sadly, building and maintaining relationships was more important than the operations. The feelings of a senior Iraqi military officer carried more weight than the lives of the soldiers whom he had put at risk by sparing the enemy and prolonging the conflict. So, he would not be found out. He would not be punished. And he would likely betray his country, and our mission, again. Although we were frustrated, this didn't come as a surprise for most of us. It turns out that I was not the only one with trust issues when it came to working with the Iraqi military.

"This is why we can't tell the Iraqis shit," someone commented, clearly discouraged.

We were more careful about how much information was shared after that. A few corrupt leaders can be mitigated, even rooted out. However, more systemic issues soon surfaced. Eventually, a unit's single cowardice response to a simple engagement caused me to completely lose faith in the Iraqi military's ability to defend their country as we had to forcibly recall some of the vehicles we had previously gifted them.

CHAPTER 16

Vehicle Recall

It didn't matter what equipment or training we gave them; the Iraqis had no desire to fight.

I was never impressed with the Iraqi military. I had seen their training and even led it. As a junior officer in 2011, I deployed alongside a team of field-grade officers who partnered with an Iraqi headquarters in central Baghdad to advise and assist their leadership. This allowed me to work with a handful of Iraqi staff officers, an infantry platoon, and the security guards of a military prison. Working with the Iraqi officers was frustrating, and I was glad we were ending our commitment to their nation after my first deployment. Or so I thought.

They didn't want our help then, just our stuff. If only they knew that war was on their doorstep, waiting for us to leave. Most of my encounters with these officers revolved around their need for me to provide them with things for free. They always wanted to know if I would be willing to give them Army boots, electronics, or even just food from our side of the base. It was the same with more senior officers, just to a higher degree, who often made outlandish demands and expected the US Army to buy their friendship.

This relationship shifted dramatically in the fight against ISIS. We were no longer a burden for them to bear or people they could take advantage of to satisfy their greed. We had transitioned from occupier to savior, and they were open and candid about their predicament. As much as I may have disliked the Iraqi senior military officers for many reasons, the ones at Union III were grateful for our help and made sure we knew, even if some of them weren't really on our side. Many of them were acutely aware of their nation's situation and showed their appreciation at every chance. Without our technology, our tools of war, they were doomed.

However, while we maintained most of the strike capabilities, the United States had previously provided the Iraqi military with a lot of equipment for conducting land warfare. They had fielded numerous types of armored vehicles designed to fight modern armies and maintained a significant technological advantage over anything ISIS could bring to the fight. While less useful in the congested urban fight—especially when we were willing to destroy any enemy stronghold they came across—these assets were essential for the Iraqi forces that operated in more open terrain.

On one hot Middle Eastern morning, I finally saw this conventional clash of armies in the desert. Even with my low expectations of the Iraqi military, I was shocked at how poorly the battle unfolded.

I had just sat down at my station, ready to eat an unhealthy amount of food for breakfast, when the US Army colonel who worked next door burst into the strike cell. "We've got trouble! An Iraqi unit got ambushed and is taking an ass whooping. People are freaking out next door."

Unbeknown to us, Iraqi forces were under attack and they had no coalition air support. They were taking losses, and the senior Iraqi officers at Union III were in a panic. The colonel relayed the information to the strike cell and we repurposed a drone to assess the situation. By the time we got our eye in the sky, the battle was already a disaster.

The tactical situation didn't really matter much to us. Personally, I didn't care how the desert engagement began; I only cared that there was a problem we needed to remedy. It appeared that ISIS fighters had ambushed an Iraqi movement. It shouldn't have been that concerning, though. The dismounted extremists were no match for the US-made armored vehicles the Iraqi military was using. It should have been an incredibly one-sided engagement. But I was very quickly proven wrong. Once again, I was reminded "should" is a terrible planning word, and I felt stupid to have bet on the Iraqi military. The only thing they consistently accomplished was letting us down.

"Why aren't they fighting back?" the director asked aloud to nobody in particular.

"I'm not sure they know how," someone replied. We all had a few good laughs. Needless to say, we didn't have much respect for the Iraqi military. And why should we, with all that we had seen from our little ivory tower?

It was strange to watch the soundless engagement. The battlefield was eerily still but somehow also chaotic. The Iraqi military had frozen, a tactical disaster against an aggressive foe. The vehicles remained static where there should have been maneuvering, and they weren't laying down any suppressive fire against the enemy. ISIS fighters began advancing, and the situation was going to go from bad to worse in the next couple of minutes.

The engagement was too fluid for us to use HIMARS. It's hard for me to admit, but the system does have its flaws. There was no guarantee any target I fired at would still be there in the few minutes it would take for the rockets to arrive. Not to mention that I couldn't hit moving targets, forcing me to saturate the area and potentially strike an ally. Because of these reasons, rocket artillery was not an option. To make matters worse, the drone we had on station was unarmed. Aircraft were on the way, but the Iraqis needed to fight independently until they arrived. Luckily, our teammates had the upper hand. Small-arms fire was bouncing off their vehicles, unable to penetrate the armor of the US-made vehicles.

Then, just before the aircraft radioed into the strike cell that they were close enough to provide support, the Iraqi military ran. The Iraqi soldiers didn't drive away or maneuver to a better position; they physically abandoned their vehicles and scattered. It was like watching an ancient battle where one side breaks in the face of an enemy charge. However, the enemy fighters didn't pursue them. They had won the contest and, with it, a significant prize as an assortment of US-made military equipment was left intact and readily available.

The enemy took over the vehicles as quickly as the Iraqis abandoned them. It was clear our mission had just shifted. Instead of enabling a victory by engaging the enemy fighters, we had to do our best to salvage the defeat and minimize the enemy's gains. Losing this much equipment was terrible. Having it turned against other friendly forces in the area would be catastrophic.

The director looked to the front row, "No squirters! Not a single vehicle gets away, ALO. I want to end this now before it becomes a bigger problem. How much time until the aircraft are ready?"

"They'll be in range to strike any second, sir," the air-liaison officer replied. "We've already briefed the pilots and divvied up the targets. We won't give them a chance to use their new toys." There were pretty good odds we would be able to destroy all the lost vehicles before they cleared the area.

However, before we dropped the first bomb, our favorite colonel burst in again, relaying a different type of panic. "Don't destroy them!" We all froze, confused.

The loss of combat power was devastating for the Iraqi unit. Still, the Iraqis at Union III were confident they could get the vehicles back. We were dramatically less confident and unclear as to exactly how they planned to accomplish such a feat after witnessing the embarrassing battle that had just occurred. Sadly, instead of destroying the lost assets, our task became watching and tracking their movements, allowing other Iraqi forces in the area to converge on the new targets.

However, the vehicles started driving off in every direction as if the plan was simultaneously being briefed to the enemy. Fun fact: it very well might have been, we had at least one traitor in the Iraqi operations center. The ISIS fighters knew they were being watched and gambled that we couldn't track all of them.

They were right. The enemy was learning.

"Darn it!" The director let out an uncharacteristic outburst. But it was so strange to hear a grown man, a stone-cold warfighter, use the same expletives as a second grader. "We need to stay with as many as we can, get me everything in the area. All other missions are cancelled. Our objective for the day is to make sure we don't lose track of any of these vehicles."

It took only a short time for the Iraqis in the operations center to reach the same conclusion we had made at the time of the incident: these vehicles wouldn't be recovered. Begrudgingly, they conceded their mistake and asked us to remove the enemy's new toys from the battlefield. We were given permission to destroy any of the vehicles we could locate.

We immediately engaged the few we had been able to follow. From there, it became a game of cat and mouse.

Identifying a single armored vehicle speeding down empty roads would be easy. But the enemy was more intelligent than that. Instead of trying to outrun our aerial sensors, they did the best thing you could do with a new treasure; they hid it. We only found some of the vehicles over the next few days. I was a spectator for most of this fiasco. Only one of these mattered to me, the one they let me engage with HIMARS.

It took hours of searching before we stumbled onto one of their hiding spots. The armored vehicle was parked under a makeshift carport—four posts and a wood slab—not so different from where we parked our HIMARS launchers. It was not 100 percent clear what the vehicle was, but it appeared to be some variant of an armored security vehicle the US Army's military police often used in Iraq, one we had probably gifted them many years prior. The vehicle was uniquely shaped, with four large wheels and a boat-like frame that made it look like it was designed to be amphibious. However, while the vehicle itself looked silly, its turret didn't. This was a significant combat multiplier for ISIS and it needed to be destroyed.

It was a straightforward mission. There were no enemy fighters around to suddenly drive the vehicle away, so we didn't have to rush. At the same time, we needed to keep the aircraft option available for the next mission in case we found a vehicle on the move. Because HIMARS can't hit a moving target, this was the best chance to save our bombs. All these arguments, made very loudly by yours truly, allowed me to beat out the Air Force officer for the opportunity to strike. He was not happy but conceded the points. His team was plenty busy that day.

I planned the mission with two rockets. The first would destroy the carport and clear a path. The second, programmed with the same coordinate but at a lower altitude, would strike the vehicle. Both had a point-detonation fuze to maximize destruction upon impact. Additionally, because I wanted the effects to happen sequentially instead of simultaneously, I had one launcher fire both rockets, creating about a three-to-five-second interval between the explosions. The plan went perfectly, but the mission was an utter failure.

After spending hours hunting these vehicles, the interest in finally seeing their demise extended beyond strike-cell personnel, drawing in some other senior officers to watch the show, albeit from the sidelines. No role, no seat.

It was a chance to once again highlight my asset. Both rockets left the launcher without incident, and then we played the waiting game, explaining to onlookers why it took so long and briefing them on the plan. The Air Force officer had wanted the target; we had some back-and-forth trash talking mid-flight, putting on a little show for the visitors. The first rocket obliterated the roof of the carport, just as planned. The second rocket followed in its wake, striking the armored vehicle perfectly with a near-vertical trajectory.

"Got 'em! Direct hit!" I hollered, excited about the successful strike. I was continually impressed with the accuracy of the rockets. We literally struck a vehicle dead center on its roof from roughly fifty kilometers away. It had a decent impact, scattering a lot of dust and smoke. Some more trash talking commenced. It felt good to show the Air Force what the Army could do. However, I quickly discovered my celebration was wildly premature.

"Ha! That still looks drivable," our Air Force officer said with a huge grin after the smoke cleared. "It was a cute little explosion, though."

While there was no evidence a carport ever existed, the vehicle seemed just fine. I was furious. And to be honest, a little embarrassed. HIMARS had incredible accuracy but just wasn't as powerful as most of us assumed it was. In fairness, there may have been some damage to the vehicle, and I definitely wouldn't have wanted to be inside it when the rocket hit. But, overall, the armored vehicle took that rocket like a champ. It probably was still drivable, but I didn't concede that point to my rival.

I was not the only one who was upset. We had wasted ammunition. The director turned toward our Air Force officer and his team and begrudgingly committed more resources to the vehicle's destruction. When they proposed a 500-pound bomb, the director looked in their direction and simply said, "Bigger." The 1,000-pound bomb they eventually dropped was overkill. Vehicle parts were scattered in every direction, leaving no doubt the target was destroyed.

The air liaison smiled at me after obliterating the target: "That's how you prosecute a target."

There was no comparison. My rockets were just not the same as Air Force bombs, especially when it came to what the munitions could destroy. I felt emasculated. I had to admit that while HIMARS was a great tool, the system was not without limitations.

CHAPTER 17

All That and a Bag of Chips

It was hard to see my asset fail … for me to fail.

When I deployed in 2016, I had an inflated sense of what HIMARS rockets could do. In the Army, we discuss rocket artillery as the ultimate combat enabler. It was the grid-square killer, capable of raining down thousands of bomblets across the battlefield. In the First Gulf War, the Iraqis had deemed it "steel rain," a horrifying and deadly experience for anyone unlucky enough to have rockets fired in their direction.

Artillery has long been the "King of Battle" or the "Last Argument of Kings," but there was a uniqueness to the steel rain. My unit had embraced it wholeheartedly, as did many others. During one of my assignments, when saluting a senior officer, subordinates expected to have their "Deep Steel!" sound off returned by the officer being saluted with a hearty "Nothing but the Rain!" This lethality is part of these units' identities, ingrained into rocket-artillery soldiers from their enlistment.

Our pre-deployment training reinforced the idea we were the Army's premier killing tool. When we supported a rotation at NTC, we simulated firing dozens of cluster-munition rockets—a tank-killing variant the Army hadn't fired since the beginning of the war over a decade prior. Because these training events simulated rocket-artillery support, it was easy to forget the weapon's purpose had changed and evolved. In the Gulf War, these cluster munitions had made rocket artillery a staple of mechanized warfare. The 2003 invasion of Iraq provided another opportunity, and the success of these destructive cluster-munition rockets against enemy armored vehicles cemented the role of rocket artillery in supporting Army divisions.

Fast forward to 2016, and rocket artillery was no longer the destructive asset it once was. While we prepared to litter the battlefield with anti-tank and anti-personnel bomblets in our work up for the war, we only used precision low-collateral-damage rockets when deployed. This was not a surprise; it had been the standard for years. Our preparation was a prime example of the Army training for the war it wanted to fight, not the one it found itself in.

Worse, when we fired rockets in training, they were reduced-range practice rockets. This special non-explosive round didn't travel far, nor did it mirror any fire-mission processing tasks needed for a precision strike. Instead, these training rockets were fired over the side of the cab like the anti-tank Cold War-era rockets they were designed to imitate. This was the rocket I fired as a young cadet at Fort Sill, Oklahoma.

In contrast, the precision rockets we used in Iraq were designed to be fired over the top of cab, with the launcher parked facing toward its target instead of perpendicular to it. While the mechanics of the rockets launch didn't really affect the crew, the process for employing the two rockets is drastically different. This was one of the main reasons we were not prepared to process fire missions when I first arrived in Iraq. Everything we had trained to do was different than what was expected. Some of these differences were minor, while others, like how we input the two mission types into our fancy artillery computer, required retraining.

Still, precision rockets are expensive and difficult to make, so it makes sense they are generally reserved for actual combat operations. However, because we never practiced with the real thing, we didn't know the limitations of the guided rockets we would use for combat. In turn, every fire mission helped us validate our assumptions and learn the reality of the weapon's capabilities.

Many of the leaders I advised associated HIMARS with the rockets of the past or believed what they had experienced at a combat training center mirrored reality. Sometimes, even if I knew the mission would fail, it was difficult to convince those around me. Because we fired over 500 rockets during my 2016 deployment to Iraq, we dealt with our fair share of unsuccessful missions. This provided the strike cell with an appreciation for the system's limitations. Still, the lessons were learned the hard way, albeit in a one-sided conflict with minimal risk to any US personnel. These challenges fit into two distinct categories: range and destructive capacity.

The system's range limitations are not a secret; anyone can look them up online. When doing so, most people only focus on how far the rockets can fly when fired, which is around seventy kilometers. While this range is incredible in a tactical fight, it's hardly sufficient for supporting operations nationwide. The system can fire a longer-range missile with a roughly 300-kilometer maximum range, but these were held in reserve for emergencies.

It's funny, and kind of sad, that because the Iraqi military was the only force generally at risk, situations didn't meet the emergency criteria often. Only having a single firing point and being restricted with travel meant there were areas I simply couldn't target with HIMARS. More firing points would eventually be added, but potential strike areas for rocket artillery remained relatively small.

While maximum range is the metric most used when describing a munition's range, only some people realize there is also a minimum effective range. For our rocket artillery, these minimum and maximum ranges are flexible depending on the altitude of both the target and the firing point. My general rule of thumb was that if the fancy artillery computer said the rocket could do it, it could. However, I failed to consider whether the rocket could do it well enough to accomplish the mission when pushing the system to its limits. The first time one of my missions failed because of range was early in the deployment.

"Is it too close for rockets?" the strike-cell director asked nobody in particular. Heads turned in my direction for input.

We identified a target uncomfortably close to the HIMARS firing point. We had received intelligence that morning that the enemy was storing weapons and ammunition in a small building roughly fifteen kilometers from Al Asad Air Base, the same place where the HIMARS launchers were stationed. If ISIS was planning a strike or a coordinated attack, this building would be an excellent forward-positioning location.

Our aircraft were conducting shaping operations elsewhere, and the drones didn't carry the firepower to destroy the building. Options were limited.

I ran the numbers, and the fancy artillery computer said the mission was feasible. "Technically, we can shoot it. But I don't know how effective the strike will be," I answered. Always undersell. The truth was, I had no idea what would happen at such a short distance.

This was not the type of mission we had used rockets for before. Our comfort zone was between 25 and 55 kilometers. In this ideal-range window, the rocket has time to reach a stable flying altitude. Additionally, when it transitions to its final-attack descent, the rocket can travel nearly straight down, significantly improving the munition's accuracy. At the maximum range, this descent is extended, and the rocket follows more of a ballistic trajectory as it fights for every extra kilometer. In contrast, for a target at minimum ranges, the rocket doesn't have time to climb, forcing it to fly a suboptimal flight path more like a straight shot.

We had missed targets before, but only ever by a little. A meter here or two meters there, and the rocket might miss the building. With a vertical descent, that means you only miss the target by a couple of meters. Near the minimum range, with the flatter flight path, a small mistake would be quickly compounded.

We built the mission and decided to take our chances. Everyone in the room was tracking that we were pushing the system's limits. We established two aim points near the center of the building and prepared for the worst. Conveniently, this mission had a speedy flight time, and I hardly required any airspace, so it didn't take long to see how it would work out.

"Shit!" I yelled as the first rocket flew right past the building. We hardly saw what happened with how fast the rockets flew at that angle, but it was clear there was a problem. The first rocket was too high, just missing the building.

The second rocket did the trick, though. While not rubble, the rocket did enough damage that nobody could hide things in the building anymore. "Hey, fifty percent man, not bad," the air-liaison officer added. "At least you still destroyed it." He was always ready to throw those jabs. In his defense, I was quick to do the same.

The rocket that missed the target went long. In fact, it went dramatically longer than what is accounted for with acceptable or expected error. Luckily, it landed in the middle of the desert and exploded harmlessly; we knew it could have been a lot worse if the target was in a town. I don't think we would have taken such a high risk if that was the case, though.

In the strike cell, the miss was funny. We all laughed at how the rocket soared over the target. A few jokes were made at my expense, particularly from my Air Force brethren. Still, the mission was a success, and we caught a lucky break in that the stray rocket didn't cause any collateral damage or, worse, kill an innocent person.

But the statistical anomaly didn't go unnoticed. Many questions were raised about the mission from outside agencies and my numerous bosses concerning the potential risks of firing HIMARS at future short-range targets. Rather than risk the administrative headache of dealing with a stray rocket again, we established a new operating procedure: no HIMARS missions closer than twenty kilometers unless it was an emergency. As already noted, Iraqi lives rarely constituted an emergency. Overall, this failure was minimal as the building was destroyed. The next failure was worse, causing nearly zero destruction and embarrassing me in the process.

We didn't often have any type of crisis, particularly one that involved HIMARS. A few times, someone from the strike cell sent a runner to find me when I was off shift, pulling me out of the gym or my room to weigh in on a topic or discuss the feasibility of doing something unique with the system. But these matters were often less pressing than the runner would make it seem.

While every day probably felt like a crisis for the Iraqi military, only one forced me to run to the office—although it, too, turned out to be overinflated.

"Sir, the director sent me to find you," a messenger said as he found me. He was out of breath and clearly frustrated. "They need you back in the strike cell like time now."

I looked at the messenger and expressed none of the urgency he was probably expecting. "Okay, give me a minute to finish this really quick," I replied. He had found me in the dining facility, grabbing a to-go plate to eat back at my station. I don't mess around when it comes to food. Plus, the dining facility is buffet style, so I always ate like a king.

"It's important, sir. Everyone is standing by waiting for you," he added. "There's a bunch of dudes in the strike cell I don't know and they're saying we need HIMARS right away. I'm not sure what it's about exactly, but they seemed pretty serious, and the director told me to emphasize that he needed you 'immediately,' no matter what you were doing."

"Well, I'm glad you didn't catch me taking a shit," I replied, only half joking.

"Sir?" he said confused. It was clear he was getting upset, and for a good reason. In his eyes, I was simply being a jerk, ignoring the orders of a superior officer. But he didn't understand the context and the complicated nature of my relationship with the director, who was quick to send a random runner with often less than urgent news. But that wasn't the messenger's fault.

"All right," I said finally. "Let's go win the war." I abandoned my lunch, which was not something I was happy about, and hustled back to the strike cell. I instantly noticed a group of officers I didn't recognize huddled near my station. Something was actually wrong.

"We need you to crater a road," the director said when he saw me come in.

I couldn't help but laugh, and replied less professionally than was appropriate when I finally composed myself. "That's a terrible idea. They're not that kind of rocket."

My rockets were explicitly designed to limit collateral damage, not create unnecessary destruction. I told him as much, explaining this was not a movie and that he would be disappointed with the results.

"They disagree," the director said, gesturing to a group of officers who didn't belong, people whom I hadn't met before.

One of these random officers I didn't know chimed in, providing a situation update to put the mission in perspective. Apparently, there was credible evidence that a massive vehicle-borne improvised explosive device (VBIED), a homemade car bomb often driven by a suicide bomber, was headed toward one of the Iraqi military units we actually cared about. For some misguided reason, numerous senior officers believed rocket artillery was the answer.

"They can disagree all they want. It doesn't make them any less wrong," I said, drawing some frowns from our visitors. "Not only will it not work, but it's also a waste of rockets." It was a terrible mission design, but that didn't matter. They had a vision in their heads about what rockets could do, a misconception about the incredibly destructive power of HIMARS, the infamous grid-square killer. So, I lost the debate. I might have been there as the subject-matter expert, but I was still only a captain. In the hierarchal world of the military, rank means everything, and I was near the bottom of that totem pole. It didn't matter if I was right.

No other assets were available, and the mission had to happen immediately, or some of our teammates were likely to die. It's funny, that typically didn't bother anyone all that much. I never figured out why this day was different. The rest of the strike cell had already found the area of the road that needed to become impassable and looked to me for a weaponeering solution. It turned out everyone really was waiting for me.

Even though I was frustrated, I still gave it the old college try and generated a mission with three rockets. I assigned the first two rockets a delay fuze to break up some of the road and the third rocket a point-detonating fuze to expand the damage. It briefed well, and nobody questioned it. Why would they? I was "the rocket guy," after all.

In a simulator or at a training center, we may have obliterated the road. I would have been the hero of the battle. But we weren't in a simulator, and this wasn't a movie. Back in the real world, I just embarrassed myself.

Both launchers were involved in the mission. I intended to have the delay fuze rockets land at the same time, with the point-detonating fuze following in their wake three to four seconds behind. We watched intently as the two rockets fell from the sky. One of the rockets functioned as expected, blasting up dust and smoke. The other failed, crunching into the asphalt, destroying itself without a blast, and sending rocket parts all over the street. It turns out it's hard to burrow into asphalt. The final rocket landed before the smoke cleared, striking right between the first two with an impressive explosion.

I couldn't help but laugh when the smoke cleared. However, I was the only one. "Well, that went about as well as could be expected."

The road was no worse than it had been 10 minutes prior. There was maybe one small pothole from the delayed round, but it wasn't big enough to deter a vehicle. In fact, most drivers probably wouldn't even avoid it. The big explosion had left some discoloration on the pavement, which was clearly superficial. If anything, the remnants of broken rockets would slow traffic more than any damage the rockets caused. While I found the failure humorous, the strike director didn't. The incoming VBIED remained a problem, but that was a problem for someone else. We never heard about some catastrophic attack on the Iraqi military in the area, making me think the intelligence was not as credible as it seemed.

There were other instances where HIMARS rockets didn't pack the punch I expected or were slightly off course. Still, the system performed magnificently throughout my deployment, and I was not the only one to think so. Luckily, when we did have these hiccups or waste ammunition on a poorly thought-out mission, there were no distinguished visitors in the room—a surprisingly common occurrence.

CHAPTER 18

Thanks For Stopping By

*I'm sure they were important people. But I didn't care;
they were generally just in the way.*

The strike cell was a popular place. From senior military officers to politicians, any dignitary who took the trip to Iraq made their way through my shop. Every guest left with a story, a video of destruction or death to tell their friends about when they returned home. Some visitors engaged us, asking questions about what we did and how we liked working in the strike cell. Others stood awkwardly in the corner, taking it all in. The worst were the ones who wanted to weigh in on a mission, adding their two cents to a developing situation or politicizing what we were doing over there.

Because of the classification of the strike cell, only a few nations could send visitors. Still, we received a diverse group of guests throughout my time there. I didn't generally take notice when someone arrived unless they approached my station. Instead, we kept working when guests entered, and there was never any announcement or planned presentation. People came to see us in action, to see the infamous screens, and to appreciate the destructive might of our military from a safe and comfortable vantage point.

Senior military officers were the bulk of the visitors. General officers in varying uniforms frequently came in, attached to our one-star on a guided tour. Rarely were they all that interested in what we were doing. This was not their first war; they had been there and done that. Instead, these officers remained on the side, discussing things of great importance. That is what I always assumed, anyway. I didn't know most of them—personally or by reputation. Many in my profession might find that odd. I have worked with a handful of mid-grade officers who track generals and admirals like they are professional athletes or celebrities, treating potential officer moves like trade rumors in the National Football League. For me, they were just another group of people passing through, some with an occasional HIMARS question.

These military visits increased dramatically in the spring of 2016 after President Barrack Obama issued an executive order to create the Operation *Inherent Resolve* Campaign Medal. It was a new piece of chest candy to wear on the uniform, a way to distinguish oneself from other people who didn't participate in the war. The military is all about sporting that flair, peacocking with tabs and badges.

Contrary to some previous campaign medals, this new ribbon required recipients to physically be in Iraq or Syria. It wouldn't be awarded to people stationed in supporting countries like Kuwait, Jordan, and Oman, even if their mission directly supported Operation *Inherent Resolve*. However, the required time they needed to spend in Iraq or Syria was only 30 days, and this could be accumulated nonconsecutively. So, anyone stuck in Kuwait who had enough pull suddenly had important business in Iraq.

Of the dozens of senior officers that came through, only one warranted shutting down operations. But this wasn't because of his rank or to allow us to put on a dog and pony show. Instead, it was because he wasn't allowed in.

About halfway through my deployment, a top French military officer paid us a visit, and he was determined to talk with the strike-cell team. France's absence from the Five Eyes intelligence alliance is a political issue I don't plan on addressing in these ramblings. It is a unique topic worth examining for those concerned with coalition warfare. At my level, it simply meant that the French, or any other ally for that matter except the United Kingdom, Australia, New Zealand, and Canada, didn't enter the strike cell. But, on this day, we made an exception and shut down our classified networks. However, we did keep the radios on in case an important mission popped up that we needed to address quickly.

We shut down nine of our televisions—leaving a random sporting event on number 10—and closed all the laptops. The French general took it in stride, laughing at the situation as he walked into the sterilized room. France was a primary coalition nation; his pilots were essential to our success. In fact, they were flying that day, making the awkward scenario humorous as he wasn't allowed to view the feed from his own aircraft if we pulled it up. He had every right to be frustrated. Instead, he maintained a positive attitude.

He wanted to meet our joint terminal attack controllers and ask them about the quality of his pilots and the integration of French aircraft. The French Mirage aircraft had performed admirably in my time in Iraq; our team let him know it. After everyone exchanged pleasantries, he allowed us to return to business, shook all our hands, and thanked us for our actions. It wasn't much, but it was memorable. It was weirdly comical to see someone with so many stars be treated like an outsider and handle it with a big smile. It was good to see humility in such a senior military officer.

While civilian visitors were less common, they were more fun than our military guests. They seemed to care more about what we were doing and were not afraid to ask any and all questions. These were not pop quizzes designed to stump us or show off how smart they were; they generally wanted to know something or were confused. Sometimes, it was as simple as getting one of us to define all the acronyms we casually threw around. If you are not used to it, military babble quickly turns into a foreign language with all the acronyms.

The HIMARS questions were generally the same regardless of who approached the desk. "What does HIMARS stand for?" "How many rockets can it hold?" "Can you fire nuclear rockets?" That last one is always a scary thought. No. The answer is no, and I hope it remains that way forever. I have studied the madness that was the 1950s Pentomic Era and am comfortable stating it should never be repeated. "What's the difference between a rocket and a missile?" This is actually a surprisingly controversial topic that depends on your military background. At a minimum, these icebreakers got them in the door and let me or some other random military officers feel comfortable talking to a civilian bigwig.

They were often people of influence. I didn't know many of them, but I understood basic titles. The preponderance of them were either politicians from varying countries or Defense Department executives. Many were senior service executives, people whose titles began with "the honorable," and elected officials from numerous countries who wanted to know more about HIMARS. However, I only had one big mission occur in front of dignitaries, one chance out of hundreds of missions to put the system on display before senior interlopers from the real world.

"Possible VBIEDS, let's start generating some options," the director announced. We had identified a shipping container in the middle of nowhere with some people coming in and out. After further observation, we discovered what appeared to be two vehicles inside. Our logical conclusion was that they were transforming them into bombs. If we didn't know what was going on, we generally assumed they were making bombs. Most of the time, they probably were.

It was a static target and would remain so for the foreseeable future, so I worked up a HIMARS weaponeering solution. "I got a two-rocket solution ready to go. Delay fuzes, one for each car. It should be a big boom." The idea was that the delay fuzes would allow the rockets to drive into the container and explode when they hit the vehicles. The targeting officer and I placed the aim points on top of where we thought the center of each car was. I got the green light and started running the show. When a HIMARS mission was occurring, I owned that room. Part of that was because it was my mission. Part of it was my personality.

Two older gentlemen stood on the side of the room by the entrance, watching me take over the strike cell. I didn't know who they were, nor did I care; I was in the zone once the missions started. We went through the normal processes. We cleared airspace, I moved the launchers to the firing point, and then I looked to the director for final approval as the other members of the team did their part to ensure it was a good strike. However, moments before we got the green light, an Allied aircraft disregarded our airspace-control measure and crossed our hotwall, freezing our operation.

I lost it, and that inappropriate language that bothered our strike director so much resurfaced. While I knew there would be a post-mission counseling, I didn't care in the moment. We quickly resolved the issue and fired both rockets. Because of the airspace issue, I was overly aggressive and ran the rest of the mission with gusto, screaming "shot" and "splash," killing any attempt at side conversations. I get excited; these missions kept my motivation level up. I have also been told that sometimes I get a little aggressive.

The explosion was perfectly placed. The shipping container was shredded, vehicle parts were scattered, and we made a hole in the desert. My motivation carried. I was proud and loud, slapping backs and messing with our airspace manager. I also threw my regular jabs toward the air-liaison officer, keeping our rivalry alive. Then, just after the smoke cleared, two people crawled out of the hole.

Impossible! We all stood there, speechless. It didn't make sense. The vehicles didn't survive the blast; how could a person? One stumbled away and started jogging. The other looked to the sky like he was looking right at us, knowing he was being watched. He reached his left hand across his body and dusted his shoulder off. It was unreal. It felt like we were watching a movie.

"Fucking zombies!" I blurted it out, not thinking, frustrated that someone had somehow survived such a perfect mission. I followed that up with some pretty vulgar expletives before screaming it again and rambling about why these people wouldn't just do us a favor and die. Our new one-star general found the whole engagement comical, laughing off on the side with our guests. The strike director, however, was livid with my outburst. The sheer unprofessionalism regarding how I talked had clearly pushed him over the edge. He very calmly walked from his station to mine and, as quietly as he could, began the usual tongue-lashing.

Apparently, my attitude had embarrassed the strike cell in front of our new general and what turned out to be a very important civilian leader in the Defense Department. But before we could argue about why officers don't use curse words, one of the older gentlemen sauntered over to our position, presumably to discuss the mission.

From the onset, he was obviously not offended or upset. In fact, he was ecstatic. With a big grin, he gave me a hearty pat on the back and said he loved my enthusiasm, the motivation was contagious, and the mission was exciting. He told me what he did for the Defense Department, shook my hand, and encouraged me not to let anyone take away my spark. Defeated, the strike director let the argument die, a battle for another day.

Of all the visitors we had in the strike cell, one civilian stood out among the crowd. Partly because we all recognized him, and partly because it was a unique experience.

A prominent US senator visited one day, garnering attention as he made his rounds. Initially, his visit was the same as the rest. He shook hands, asked questions, thanked us for our service, and exchanged pleasantries. Then he was off to the next appointment, a man with a schedule and a team to keep him on it. However, distinct from his predecessors, he came back.

One of the senator's aides returned to the strike cell shortly after leaving. Apparently, the rest of the tour had not been as engaging as our little war room. While there was plenty of time for meet and greets as the trip continued, the aide asked if the senator could spend some quality time with the strike-cell crew, gaining firsthand mission experience. We gave him a chair in the center row next to one of the battle captains. The day was not chaos by any means, but we found action. It was generally easy to find missions when we went looking for something to destroy.

By choosing to take a seat with us instead of standing on the side, he stopped being a visitor. Instead, he was part of the team, albeit only for a short time. So, we put him to work. He weighed in on missions, cheered the successes, and felt our frustrations as we worked through everyday challenges. There were no politics and no photo opportunities. Just people. It was a genuine shared moment. It was refreshing to see a political figure as just a man. Hopefully, it was enriching for him to share in our experience, allowing him to see us in a new light.

Not every guest was lucky enough to spend the day hunting ISIS with our crew. In fact, some spent barely a few minutes in the strike cell. During the peak of an Iraqi counteroffensive, it didn't matter when a visitor entered, the action was afoot, and missions were aplenty. However, the place could be pretty dull in transition, with nine screens viewing the desert or a ghost town in central Iraq. Luckily, we stayed prepared to show off our greatest hits.

While our televisions were live feed, which I had previously discovered were on varying degrees of delay, we also received footage of most of the strikes. For HIMARS strikes, this sometimes allowed me to make a storyboard PowerPoint presentation to send to the team at the firing point or to the rest of the artillery battalion back in Kuwait and the United States. While great for sharing, rarely were they worth a rewatch or showing to visitors. I was still proud of them, though. On the other hand, the more dynamic strikes often led to unique situations. Situations that you had to see to believe.

Sadly, we liked to watch these videos and share them with others. So, we made a highlight reel. I'm not proud to have been a part of this. I don't feel good that we did it. Still, it happened. We used it as a tool to showcase some positive and negative weapon characteristics. For example, we often showed visitors the precision of the laser-guided air-to-ground Hellfire missile as it was expertly guided through a window or hit a motorcycle on the move.

There is one of these highlight videos that I still think about, one that I'm sad to say I laughed at on numerous occasions.

A group of ISIS fighters was congregating on and around a brick wall. In our eyes, they were planning something. In reality, they were probably just enjoying each other's company and getting some rest. Regardless, they were armed enemy forces in hostile territory and a valid military target. While they may not have seemed like a threat at the time, it was a fluid battlefield. It's not a stretch to think they would be engaging our Iraqi military partners in the near future.

We sent a Hellfire into the group's center to scatter them and remove as many as possible. The blast was minimal, killing a few and maiming others. The rest ran. Nothing out of the ordinary. Nothing to write home about. Then, one got up. Something like that had happened numerous times throughout the deployment, and I continued to be impressed with some people's will to live.

The man in question leaped to his feet, alert and afraid. Without thinking or assessing his surroundings, he ran. His instincts took over and he just ran. He ran at full speed for about ten yards and then crashed face first into the wall his comrades had been sitting on. Another minute or so went by and he regained his composure, slowly standing up and walking toward safety, clearly disoriented and likely concussed.

What a stupid thing for him to do. We laughed. Between clip shows and YouTube, society has trained us to find videos like this comical. It was such a unique experience for us to witness. We continued laughing. We joked, poking fun at this man's decision making and making fun of his fight-or-flight response. We added it to the reel. We shared it with visitors. We laughed some more. It was one of our favorites, playing dozens of times throughout the trip.

It was terrible. We laughed at the circumstances, yes. But we also laughed at this human. He may have been our enemy, but he was suffering. We didn't know his story. This was someone's son, someone's brother. He was our enemy. He was a valid target, and I have no qualms about his potential death. But taking a life should not be so easy on the spirit; no matter its justification, killing shouldn't be a jovial event.

We dehumanized ISIS. The killing was easy. Our highlight reel grew, and visitors never left empty handed, a story or a video serving as the mementos of the trip to the strike cell. It turns out it wasn't difficult to find targets in ISIS-controlled territory. Even the simplest things can get you killed in such a one-sided conflict. However, I'm disappointed it took too long for many of us to fully appreciate the weight of what we were doing daily and remember this was not a game, even when we made it one.

CHAPTER 19

We Don't Take Kindly

One day, it just stopped being funny.

The legal justification behind taking another life is an interesting concept. We establish specific rules for engaging enemy forces as the guide for targeting, rules that are constantly reviewed and validated to ensure what we are doing is right. Some of these are obvious and uncontroversial. For example, if an enemy fighter is actively shooting their weapon at friendly forces—committing a hostile act—we are authorized to engage. At the same time, we can always defend ourselves; that is a constant across warfare and the easiest one to justify. Before my deployments, my older brother always told me it's better to be judged by 12 than carried by six, meaning it's better to pull the trigger and face a jury than to doubt a decision and get killed.

These rules were not incredibly clear my first time in Iraq. As a young lieutenant, I didn't have the necessary experience to understand the contextual nuances of applying lethal force during counterinsurgency operations. It was often hard to distinguish the enemy from the civilian population. Even if we knew someone was not on our side, that didn't necessarily mean we could kill them. We needed proof, and most decisions to take lethal action faced intense scrutiny. To be perfectly honest, I was more afraid of facing the legal consequences of having to fire my rifle at a suspected insurgent than actually facing the enemy. Thankfully, that first deployment revolved more around hypervigilance and avoiding improvised explosive devices on the side of the road than fighting enemy insurgents.

Fighting ISIS was different. They were a declared hostile force. They were also easy to find because they had control of terrain and proudly flew their black flag. This made the rules of engagement much more straightforward than my previous deployment. An adult male walking the streets of an ISIS-occupied town with a weapon on his back was an enemy. We faced little ambiguity when distinguishing friend from foe. Instead, our biggest challenge was ensuring we had the proper legal justification for striking when we identified our targets.

We all learned to talk in the legal language required to prosecute our missions. We would justify a strike by saying an ISIS fighter's action fits the rules of engagement number this or was a violation of established policy that. For strikes in support of Iraqi military offensive operations, we were straight business, ensuring rockets, missiles, and bombs were delivered safely and timely. These days were busy but rewarding. Recapturing territory provided a clear purpose that produced tangible results. Everyone inherently understood why we needed to kill the enemy fighter shooting mortars or firing a machine gun.

However, there was often a lull between offensive operations. During these more mundane times, we balanced our deliberate efforts to shape the battlefield for the next Iraqi operation with random dynamic targets in our area. When it was really slow, we searched our area for enemy forces conducting meetings or weapons training, which would get us into the fight and bring a sense of accomplishment to the day.

The rules of engagement were continually updated. While nothing ever fundamentally changed our established policies for applying force, some additions and justifications for obscure missions sometimes seemed silly. This is not because they were wrong or immoral, but because we often lacked the context behind their creation. Still, we learned who and what we could strike and where we had limitations. From there, it was a matter of hunting.

No one decided to turn these obscure strikes into a game. We never agreed to some grand idea or discussed categorizing the missions comically. One day it happened naturally, and it stuck as a running joke for most of the deployment. I'm disappointed to confess how much fun I had and how invested I was in finding a little humor in the destruction we caused. The game started after a simple mission on a slow day.

"What's with the truck?" I asked, walking back into the strike cell from lunch.

"Not sure," the director replied. "It looks like they just abandoned it out here."

One of our drones had identified a random pickup truck parked in the middle of nowhere. They had been scouring the area for a few minutes but found no sign of life, concluding it had been abandoned recently.

"All right. What are we thinking? Why is this thing parked in the middle of nowhere?" the director asked, gauging the group and trying to understand what we were looking at.

To be honest, it didn't really matter why it was there, but we decided to create some elaborate backstory to explain the circumstances. After joking about a few different narratives that could have led to this situation, our hypothetical stories regarding the truck's predicament sparked a debate concerning the possibility it was parked in a remote location to be transformed into an improvised explosive device. When you are looking for bombs, a lot of things start looking suspicious.

Naturally, we decided it needed to be destroyed. We would do our part to clean up the battlefield by removing the makeshift bomb. That is what we told ourselves, at least. We very well might have just been wasting time and ammunition, not to mention destroying some random person's truck.

There was no pressure to conduct the mission quickly; no enemy was in sight, and it was not synchronized with an Iraqi military operation. HIMARS provided a readily available answer, and it didn't take much analysis for me to decide to use a single rocket with a point-detonating fuze. It was one of the most straightforward missions of the deployment. The rocket struck the vehicle perfectly, creating a decent explosion.

We will never know whether the truck was being reconfigured as a bomb. If it was, we saved the day for some unsuspecting Iraqi military unit in the area. If it wasn't, someone lost a truck—albeit one abandoned in the desert. It was a gamble we were all comfortable with. Mission accomplished.

After the mission, we joked for a little while about some of the other narratives behind the truck's origin: "What if someone is camping? They are out there just enjoying some nature and when they come back, they find their truck in a million pieces." We all laughed a little.

Then, uttered casually from across the room, "Well, I guess you aren't allowed to go camping in Iraq." It was quite a leap, but everyone instantly appreciated the connection. In fact, a similar line of reasoning could be applied to most of our obscure missions.

Just like that, our dull days got more interesting as random missions gained some silly context. Without ever discussing it, everyone started to identify what you were not authorized to do in Iraq. For a couple of weeks, every time a strike occurred outside of actual hostilities, someone would chime in with a clever "Guess you can't do that in Iraq." We started tracking the different things, always trying to add a new one to the list and earn a few laughs, a way to lighten the mood. Sadly, a handful of these laughs were at the expense of someone's life.

Vehicles were the easiest to categorize in the game. We destroyed them for all sorts of reasons. It seemed that if ISIS had a vehicle or one happened to remain in their occupied territory, it was a readily justifiable target. We had imagined a handful of different vehicle restrictions. For example, if a vehicle fled a strike or an engagement, we would often follow it and destroy it with a Hellfire missile. We quickly established that the penalty for speeding in Iraq was death. Similar to the game's origin, we sometimes found vehicles under makeshift carports or covered with a tarp. This was likely to protect against sun damage. Less likely, but plausible, it was to hide its transformation into a bomb. If you can't tell, there was considerable fear of vehicle-borne improvised explosive devices during this time. So, no vehicle coverings were allowed in Iraq.

The game applied to people as well. After witnessing someone burying a random object (an improvised explosive device?) and receiving a Hellfire for his efforts, we joked that digging was no longer authorized. Training with a firearm? No brainer, death. No improving marksmanship on our watch. Running, especially sprinting, raised lots of questions and drew attention. Therefore, training for a race was a definite no-go and a possible way to get killed.

One day we identified two individuals carrying what appeared to be laminated paper. It was considered significant because there aren't too many lamination machines floating around Iraq. It was likely a map or a communication cheat sheet. We followed them for a while, eventually gathering enough intelligence to justify a legally approved strike. After the strike, we jokingly decreed that arts and crafts must remain an indoor activity. To bring fancy paperwork outside is to announce you are essential; vital members of ISIS needed to die.

It might seem unnecessary or a downright horrible thing to do, but the game broke up the monotony of the deployment. It helped pass the time on a slow day and kept spirits high through some challenging periods in the war. Just as important, it allowed us to step back from the gravity of what we were doing. Most of us understood this was a balancing act.

It's dangerous to altogether remove yourself from the implications of deciding to take another life, to make the process too easy. However, advancements in technology continue to make this an option. This will be exacerbated if society eventually transitions to lethal autonomous weapons that can decide to kill based on their programmed parameters, a potential future for certain parts of a chaotic battlefield.

At the same time, it's not healthy to dwell on every action, consumed with the moral conundrum of killing in the name of peace, duty, or ambiguous government objectives. I don't know how well I walked this line between the two extremes. It was simpler to err on the side of distancing myself during the deployment with the intent to subsequently examine my actions in reflection. However, sometimes the situation was too hard to ignore, too real to distance yourself from.

One day we received an updated "be on the lookout for" notice from higher up that fit perfectly into our game. We were directed to watch for ISIS members conducting river crossings, likely trying to avoid detection or smuggle weapons and supplies around the country. We received clear guidance that required us to destroy any boats making such river crossings. Barely a minute after the directive was announced to the team, someone joked: "I guess there's no fishing in Iraq."

Generally speaking, this was not a problem for rocket artillery. Not only is HIMARS unable to hit a moving target, a problem that needs to be remedied, but it's incredibly challenging to identify a good grid coordinate in a body of water. So, when we identified our first river crossing just two days later, I sat back to enjoy my role as a spectator, observing a mission I would never forget.

It was easy to catch a boat conducting a crossing. We dedicated some of our collection assets to patrol up and down the Euphrates River in our area. From identification to strike was incredibly fast. Because we used a Hellfire from the drone observing the boat, we didn't have to go through all the challenges associated with HIMARS missions, like clearing airspace, moving the launchers, and minutes of flight time for the rocket. Instead, once we got the approval—an easy process given the destruction of these boats was a directed mission—we engaged.

Laser-guided munitions are a tricky thing. Throughout the deployment, we witnessed some of the most impossible shots from the drone operators, like putting missiles through windows and hitting the front wheel of a speeding motorcycle. We also observed some surprising misses on what appeared to be a relatively easy target. Needless to say, we were on the edge of our seats for the few seconds between the release of the Hellfire and the impact.

This one was close, striking the back of the boat. It was enough to sink it, but not nearly the brutality that would have occurred if it landed in the center of the boat with the passengers. After a few seconds, a couple of survivors surfaced and prepared for a challenging swim across the Euphrates.

"There's no swimming in Iraq!" someone hollered as five ISIS fighters began their journey. Everyone laughed. When we could, we had fun. Initially, it wasn't clear if we would reengage or simply wait and follow them once they reached the other side. Then the chatter took over. We were so removed from the situation that we got caught up in our banter:

"No way they make it across."

"It's not that far, at least two or three reach the other side."

"I'll take that bet!"

A game within a game. Everybody started hollering predictions. There was little confidence that many would make the swim. In their defense, the swimmers did just survive a missile strike. It was fun at first, but the mood quickly turned dark. We all inherently knew those men were in a bad situation, and it became apparent most were unprepared for this contingency.

It didn't take long for the first one to disappear. The banter continued but on a smaller scale. Then a second swimmer went under and didn't resurface. After that, the chatter stopped, and the realization of what was happening hit. We were watching these people drown and it was unlikely any would survive. However, because fighters making it across the river had battlefield implications, we had to keep the camera on the swimmers. It became very uncomfortable. We had grown accustomed to seeing fighters killed, but not like this. It felt too real.

The situation took me back to the last day of my junior year in high school. A friend of mine, a football teammate, missed our end-of-the-year party. We ended up finding out that night he had drowned while swimming with his girlfriend. Being the resident "old man" of the friend group, I found myself having the hard conversations, telling everyone what had happened and reaching out to other people's parents. I thought a lot about what my friend went through that night, the struggle to fight for air, the realization all is lost, and the acceptance of one's fate. When I watched those fighters thrashing around in the water, these emotions from my youth, from one of my first exposures to death, resurfaced.

I was not alone. The attitude in the strike cell had shifted. You don't have to have lost a friend in the water to appreciate the torture of struggling for air and to have the realization you might not survive. It's easy to remove yourself from a situation that is hard to imagine. This may be why most of our missions didn't affect us, at least not at the time.

Few people can relate to a building suddenly exploding or rockets unexpectedly falling from the sky. In contrast, most people can appreciate the feeling of being underwater, fighting to come up for air. It's not hard for me to imagine myself in a pool, holding my breath for as long as possible. There is a weird but natural feeling of fear when you can't hold your breath anymore and are forced to resurface. We understood exactly what these people were fighting through. Because of that, this mission was the first time many of us genuinely related to our enemy. Whether we wanted to or not, it was a situation that forced us to empathize with ISIS.

There was nothing we could do to change the situation, even if we wanted to, so we just watched. Still, it pained me to see these men struggle, to fight for every breath and eventually give up, accepting the inevitable. Even though it was our job to defeat this evil force, I found myself hoping that at least one of them would overcome this obstacle.

"Don't you fucking quit," I muttered softly. The words barely escaped my lips, a whisper. However, the strike cell had grown eerily silent, so my whisper still carried. I felt the director look my way. Our eyes locked in a brief, uncomfortable moment. But he wasn't angry; he was hurting, just as I was. Instead of his typical rant about inappropriate language, he simply nodded. He didn't say it, but I think he felt the same as me. I think most of us were troubled by what the mission had become.

The ISIS swim somehow took on meaning, symbolizing the futility of our conflict. I was no longer watching the enemy. I was just watching men face adversity and, at that moment, I desperately wanted them to keep fighting and reach the shore. And I was not alone. The strike cell had gone silent, most of us standing, emotionally invested in the fate of these young men. I needed them to fight, to just not quit. We needed someone to survive.

But that was not how this day would end. There was no happy ending.

They all drowned in the river that day. One at a time, each went under, never to resurface. Not a single one came close to the refuge of the shore. Some lasted longer than others, but they all quit, each death a dagger to my heart.

The strike cell felt a little different after that. We didn't discuss what had happened, and the rest of the day was quiet. It was the first time since I had arrived that a mission impacted the group as a whole. Our game ended as suddenly as it began. It would resurface at times, but never like it was before we struck that boat.

Previously, there had been missions that led a strike-cell member to take a day or two off. Although it didn't happen often, sometimes a person stepped away, never returned, and a replacement officer took over their position. The missions impacted everyone differently, and nobody passed judgment on those who didn't wish to partake in the violence any longer. But this mission was different. There was a collective acceptance that what we saw impacted us as humans, and we needed to take a momentary pause if able.

Luckily, there were no other missions that day. Additionally, we didn't hunt like usual. Instead, we just sat quietly and waited for the day to be done. It was the first time I could reflect on what we were doing in Iraq and my role in this extermination. My eyes were opened to the horrors of our technological war; other aspects of our missions became harder to ignore.

CHAPTER 20

Mortuary Affairs

*It took me way too long to realize they were people,
human beings just like us.*

It's hard to see yourself in the enemy. It should be simple. When militaries clash, both sides are made up of brave young men and women willing to risk everything. Motivations vary not just for each side but often for each individual, including duty, religion, country, defending territory, or one of the many other reasons used to march a nation's youth off to war. Even though the combatants are pitted against each other, they are not so different at the individual level. Instead, they are just victims of their circumstances. But it doesn't feel that way; I have come to realize this is by design, that we are conditioned to see the enemy in a specific way, making it easier to kill each other.

The most difficult thing you can ask a person to do is to kill and be willing to die. This is the essence of warfare—killing and dying. In turn, a strong narrative is required to convince the masses to embark on such an endeavor. Historically, this narrative was often underlined by how awful the enemy was: barbarians who are out of control, a suppressed society that needed liberation from its oppressors, savages, or simply an evil that must be eradicated. The subsequent war propaganda often paints the enemy as less than human, a foreign monster threatening our way of life. This is not an exaggeration. During World War I, the United States depicted the Germans as monstrous monkeys with clubs, mad brutes coming for our families. In World War II, the Japanese were depicted as caricatures, exaggerating racial stereotypes in a deliberate effort to dehumanize them.

In modern times, ISIS made this narrative easy. Beyond being culturally and racially different, the organization's actions were outlandish and condemned internationally. They were the bad guys, openly committing atrocities and displaying them to the world in a misguided demonstration of their commitment to their cause. The ISIS-released execution videos replaced the propaganda posters of old, and the 24-hour news cycle did the rest. When I got to Iraq, the enemy was easy to hate. ISIS had become my generation's Nazis and had to be stopped. I was excited to do my part in eradicating them from the earth.

I could play that narrative in my head whenever things felt morally ambiguous. It was such a one-sided fight that sometimes our missions felt wrong, a technological mismatch that made any battle unfair. Still, I was comfortable with the fact we were preventing the scourge of the earth from spreading. I have often told myself we were killing in the name of peace, a necessary evil. I wonder how often this narrative has been used throughout history to convince good people to commit violence along a similar line of reasoning.

Over the course of the deployment, three missions forced me outside of this comfort zone and made me appreciate the enemy for who they were: human beings. The first time was in the river. This was the only time the actual death of enemy fighters really bothered me. As I have said before, and will continue to reinforce, these men deserved to die. I will not be convinced otherwise. ISIS would not be reasoned with; there would be no peace treaty or coexistence.

The other two missions had nothing to do with the fighters themselves. Instead, I was rattled by those who were left to clean up the mess we made of their comrades. There was something inherently disturbing about watching people care for their dead. As a soldier, mortuary affairs hit too close to home.

One afternoon, our intelligence team informed us they had located one of the senior ISIS leaders in the area. He was hosting a meeting with a handful of his team in a place we were free to destroy. We had confirmed the site was free of civilians, and it had been designated a target zone. The intelligence analysts had been watching the ISIS senior leader for some time and had just gotten the confirmation they had hoped for. We switched one of our televisions to their video feed and identified the medium-sized, perfectly square, one-story building that was our target. A couple of other buildings were nearby, but there was plenty of space between them so we didn't have to worry much about collateral damage. A perfect HIMARS mission.

I planned the mission with a three-rocket solution, all delay fuzes in a triangular pattern. The rockets hit where they were supposed to and the building collapsed into a pile of rubble. A simple and straightforward mission. We always waited a few minutes after destroying a building to see if anyone crawled out; they rarely did but, since it was a possibility, we kept watch, especially since an ISIS leader was supposedly inside. This time, something unexpected happened.

"What the hell are they doing?" someone blurted out as reinforcements rushed to the destruction before we could see if there were any survivors. People started flooding out of the other buildings. This was a first for our team. Usually, everyone ran from an explosion, not toward it. They climbed on the rubble, throwing stones off the pile in search of something. Our initial assessment was that the building must have contained critical documents or equipment for the meeting.

"Repeat!" the director yelled. Although he announced it to the group, it was aimed at me. It's an artillery command to fire the same mission again.

"On it," I replied instantly. I was able to process the mission quickly because the airspace was still clear, the launchers were already on the firing point, and a reload wasn't needed yet. "I'm shifting the fuze from delay to proximity to rain down some shrapnel. Launchers are ready, permission to reengage."

"Do it," he said, giving the final approval to strike.

Just like the first volley, the rockets struck their target perfectly. The first two burst above the target at the same time, and shrapnel rained into the rubble, killing or mortally wounding anyone who was reckless enough to have climbed onto the target area. The third exploded a few seconds later, an unnecessary addition to the carnage. Again, the onlookers didn't flee. Instead, more people came running toward the rubble. It didn't make sense. I watched, puzzled. I wasn't alone.

Some people in the strike cell started laughing, encouraging the next group to run to their deaths and joking about the idiocy of it all. It was going to be a good day for my tracker. "We could do this all day ... Drop it down to two rockets and repeat it again!" the director said, laughing. He was thinking the same as me. This was an easy win.

We definitely didn't need the third rocket. I recreated the mission in my artillery computer for two rockets. "Launchers are ready. Be advised, I'll have to pull one launcher off to reload after this mission." While each ammunition pod can hold six rockets, they aren't reloaded with individual rockets. This meant we often had strange pairings between the launchers, where one launcher would have a full pod of six rockets while the other would only have a couple. We had to balance making sure we had enough rockets loaded to always prosecute a target while also working to empty a pod to make room for new ones.

"Acknowledged. Fire when ready," he said, providing his approval.

The airspace was still clear, and I was about to give the command to fire when someone interrupted the mission and yelled over our banter "CHECK FIRING! CHECK FIRING! CHECK FIRING!"

We stopped what we were doing. I literally took a step back from my computer and raised both hands, an instinctive reaction to the familiar command that none of us ever wanted to hear. "Check firing" is the artillery command to stop everything, a command to freeze. This is often for safety reasons or serious mistakes. In this case, it was because the group that had just arrived was not digging in the rubble or searching for anything. Instead, they were tending to their fallen—wounded and dead alike. They were providing aid to those they could and conducting mortuary affairs for the others.

This fundamentally changed the tactical situation. The mission was canceled. When possible, you don't interfere with people who are taking care of the dead. Bodies were quickly organized beside the building, and the digging resumed. We watched for a while, but no documents or equipment was unearthed, only friends and brothers to be added to the pile.

Until then, we had never really considered the mortuary affairs aspect of our technological war. We were quick to kill, assess, and move on, leaving the battlefield behind us as quickly as we found it. What happened after our strikes was not our concern.

Out of sight, out of mind. That is the mantra of those not willing to deal with hard problems. Cleanup was an Iraqi problem, after all.

Not this time. While we had become desensitized to seeing the victims, this was our first time watching people grieve. The pain was palpable. These monsters cared for each other and were anguished over the loss. This new reality added an emotional layer to our actions, providing context and consequences to our missions. It was inherently human and difficult to ignore. However, we moved on quickly, both that day and in general. We avoided that situation moving forward; our job was to defeat the enemy, not sympathize with them.

A few months would pass before we would have to endure a situation like that again, this time in an area we had already systematically destroyed.

"Just received an update from intel, they're back in that same block again," the battle captain announced to the group, reading a report off his computer. "I don't get it. They must have tunnels to get between the buildings. Either that or they're just stupid and aren't learning from the previous strikes that killed their friends," he mused, providing the commentary for what we were all thinking.

A neighborhood should not become familiar to those of us conducting this technological type of warfare. We weren't walking the streets or getting to know the locals. And yet, this one stood out. Near the end of my deployment, ISIS was determined to have us destroy the same city block week after week, returning to see the neighborhood continually deteriorate each visit. I had previously destroyed three separate buildings on this quarter-mile straightaway block. Each time, an important gathering occurred that we needed to interrupt. I laughed when we heard that ISIS was having another meeting in the familiar territory.

"That's different," the director said when we got our drone overhead. It quickly became apparent this gathering was not like the others. Instead of piling into a building, a large group formed in the middle of the road. "Thoughts?"

A single Hellfire missile wouldn't do the trick. The ISIS fighters were intelligent and had spread themselves out along the street. They made small groups and kept a healthy distance from others.

They were learning.

However, unlike the insurgents we dealt with years prior, they couldn't fight back, not really. We didn't walk the streets, making ourselves targets. We sat in our tiny room by Saddam Hussein's old palace, immune to the threat. This is not to say this adjustment to how ISIS fighters gathered was not frustrating, as it dramatically limited how we could engage them. In fact, it would take more Hellfires than we had airborne to engage most of the people, and the crowd would disperse too quickly for that option either way.

Killing the group with Air Force bombs also didn't make sense, as it meant destroying a city block. But we did weigh this option. Not many were opposed to the collateral damage. In fact, because ISIS was not taking the hint in the area, there was an argument made that a massive bombardment could serve as a demonstration to other enemy fighters and motivate them to withdraw.

"Hear me out," I chimed in, breaking the awkward silence. "What if we spread out four rockets with proximity fuzes. We could have near-simultaneous effects on the whole block without unnecessarily destroying the infrastructure." I got excited about a plan coming together. "We can place the first two aim points at each end of the road, with the following two near the center of the straightaway. Shouldn't be more than a couple of seconds between the two sets of explosions, barely enough time for the guys in the middle to figure out what's going on."

The strike director gave the approval, and I started developing the rocket-artillery solution. Just like weaponeering the buildings, finding the perfect aimpoints to fire into a large crowd involved a lot of winging it. But it generally made sense, and without any objections, we moved forward. Clearing the airspace didn't take long, and I received final strike authorization before the crowd dispersed.

"Shot! All rockets fired," I announced to the group. I had successfully completed a lot of missions, but this one was unique. I was really putting the rockets to the test, seeing how they worked in a more conventional setting that required area effects as much as it did precision. It was exciting, and I knew it would be a good day for the stat tracker, regardless of how many of the enemy fighters were able to scatter between the blasts.

I watched nervously, expecting the crowd to panic, waiting to see this great statistics prize slip from my grasp as the seconds ticked away. "Hold … just another minute" I said aloud, willing them to stay in spite of the imminent danger. Luckily, there was no traitorous phone call to offer a warning while the rockets traveled to their destination. And as loud as they are, the rockets didn't spook our prey as they crept up to the crowd at supersonic speeds.

The plan worked perfectly. Two puffs of smoke appeared above the street at both ends of the road. Then, just seconds after, the next two exploded in quick succession before panic could take over and disperse the mob. Although the muted video and lack of large explosions made the whole mission anticlimactic, we instantly knew it was successful.

I was surprised at how accurate the impacts were. It was always strange seeing what I had crafted on the computer come to fruition. I was excited and other people in the strike cell were offering congratulations. Everyone knew this was a big one.

I sat for a few seconds, anxiously awaiting the damage assessment, ready to add numbers to my spreadsheet and bask in the glory of a mission well done. At a minimum, I had four rockets fired to add to the list. I just needed to wait for the smoke to clear and the bodies to be counted.

"Sir, we got an urgent observation request," the battle captain chimed in. "Iraqi ground forces are reporting movement not far from the last strike, we might have spooked some other enemy in the area."

"Don't you fucking say it!" I said under my breath. They were going to steal my drone. My mission wasn't over. I needed to know the results. I needed to see the aftermath.

"Acknowledge," the director replied. "Shift the drone from this strike for a minute; let's see what we've got going on." I don't know what sound I made in response, but it clearly relayed my frustration. "Have some patience, Brennan. Your casualties aren't going anywhere." Little did he know, the bodies would be on the move not long after the smoke cleared.

Luckily, it only took a few minutes of observing the suspected enemy activity to realize the new area was a waste of time. After accepting that the issue wasn't as urgent as the Iraqis made it seem, the drone returned to our favorite neighborhood for an official battle-damage assessment of the strike.

It was sheer carnage. Bodies littered the street, absent movement. It turns out block parties are not authorized in Iraq.

From our vantage point, it wasn't clear if any damage was done to the buildings. Nothing collapsed, but there may have been some superficial damage from the shrapnel. The people, on the other hand, didn't stand a chance. The shrapnel proved highly effective, demonstrating that precision rockets could still produce the traditional area effects often associated with artillery strikes.

We started tallying up the kills for our official battle-damage assessment but were interrupted by people coming out of some of the buildings, searching for survivors. It quickly became apparent there were very few still alive. Eventually, the newcomers started collecting the dead.

Two people pushing old rusty wheelbarrows moved through the area, providing a final ride for their fallen. I don't know where they came from, but it seemed like a battle drill for them. They had done this before and clearly knew their role in conducting the hasty mortuary affairs operation. It was such a strange sight that we couldn't help but fixate on it.

I watched, unsettled, as corpses were thrown into the wheelbarrows, lifeless limbs flopping around as the collector trudged down the road, struggling to maintain the heavy load. I didn't know it then, but that image was burned into my memory and would haunt me for years, eventually changing how I would view warfare. We stopped counting bodies and used the drone to follow one of the wheelbarrows. It took its passengers to a collection point by the river just outside the neighborhood. I didn't know their eventual plan for their dead; that was not our problem. At that moment, they just piled them up.

We had seen enough. This was the part of the battle that was best ignored. Out of sight, out of mind. The drone pilot reported the assessment and we moved on. It was one of my most successful missions, but I didn't care about the statistics at that moment. We couldn't watch anymore; there was something just uncomfortable about seeing someone care for the dead. It didn't help that we were the ones who created the mess for them to clean up. There were mixed emotions throughout the strike cell that day. While we did what needed to be done, the reality of what we were doing in Iraq and what our mission entailed was on full display. And it was difficult to face.

We checked back on our favorite neighborhood a few days later. The bodies were gone. In fact, we found no sign of life there at all. It appeared ISIS wouldn't be hosting large groupings there anymore. They had finally received the message. When Iraqi security forces returned to offensive operations in May, they eventually seized the area, finding the neighborhood deserted. The enemy had been defeated in this small part of Iraq.

We could win this war one neighborhood at a time. We owned the sky; it was a technological mismatch of extreme proportions. Realistically, there was little ISIS could do to stop us or even fight back. However, the cost wouldn't only be high for ISIS. We had created numerous abandoned neighborhoods like this one in my few months in Iraq, areas I'm not sure the population could return to for years because of the destruction. This made me wonder what would be left of Iraq when ISIS was defeated by our technical means, when we rooted out the enemy one structure at a time.

Hunting was sparse for the next couple of weeks. We had ISIS in a vice in central Iraq and continued to squeeze whenever they gave us an opportunity. After that brutal mission with proximity fuzes, ISIS gatherings in our area were few and far between. That mission would be one of my last, and it would stay with me. The war was coming to a close, at least in central Iraq, and what was left of the fight was gradually moving out of my range window.

As the summer approached, a single stronghold remained in central Iraq and ISIS began consolidating its forces wherever possible. Based on our assessment, ISIS was gearing up for the next great battle. By besieging Fallujah since February, we had forced the eventual clash of armies and chosen historical ground for them to make their stand. Fallujah is an infamous place for the US military, and a hard place for many to return to. Regardless, the siege came to its natural end as the summer began, and the Iraqi security forces began their final offensive in our area. In May 2016, we were ready to support the Third Battle of Fallujah and, by all appearances, it would mirror the previous two from a decade prior. We were ready to help the Iraqi security forces win a bloody door-to-door fight and finally expel ISIS from central Iraq.

CHAPTER 21

Exodus

It was like a video game; it was hard to believe it was real.

Very few moments from the "forever war" in Iraq stand out among the years of stability counterinsurgency operations. However, three events epitomized the intensity of the conflict and became well known outside the military community: the invasion, the surge, and the battles for Fallujah. Fallujah gained notoriety as the Marines twice fought door-to-door in 2004 in some of the bloodiest battles of the Iraq War, expelling insurgents from the town at a high cost. Images from the conflict captured the world's attention, including an iconic photo of a Marine shot while attempting to drag his wounded comrade from danger.

Fast forward to 2016 and we were headed back to Fallujah. Even in a support role, this operation took an emotional toll on many senior coalition leaders. Undoubtedly, some would likely be overjoyed to turn the town to rubble and remove it from the map.

The battle was inevitable. Everything had been building to this moment. Liberating Ramadi had reversed some of the ISIS advances and slowed their momentum. That success allowed the Iraqi military to isolate Fallujah, removing it from external support. Securing Hit and Kubaysah reduced any chance of ISIS reinforcing its isolated fighters, limited a larger reconsolidating of ISIS in Iraq, and made a potential withdrawal back to Syria incredibly challenging. We had chosen this engagement and the ground for it.

The next fight would be remembered as the Third Battle of Fallujah and will hopefully be the last in that forsaken town. Going into it, we all knew that, if it was successful, the offensive operation had the potential to destroy what strength ISIS had left in the region and effectively win the war in central Iraq.

Just before summer began in 2016, the siege on Fallujah was lifted, and the Iraqi military initiated offensive operations. The Iraqi military had a string of successes early, finding numerous outskirt neighborhoods abandoned or minimally manned. Our shaping efforts had proved fruitful. By destroying any ISIS attempts at building fortifications or fighting positions, to include killing the fighters doing the construction, coalition strikes significantly reduced the ability of ISIS to mount much of a defense.

But this didn't mean these areas were given away freely. Instead, what resistance the fighters could manage, they did. Minor skirmishes ensued, with the Iraqi military getting the better of its inferior foe. To complicate matters, ISIS left improvised explosive devices behind as they withdrew. Not only did this frustrate our Iraqi counterparts, but it slowed down operations, a delaying tactic that allowed ISIS to consolidate what few forces remained into Fallujah proper.

The battle intensified over the next few weeks. As the Iraqi military moved into the city, they faced stiff resistance. At the same time, coalition strikes became limited by the presence of so many civilians. There were a few exciting moments when we isolated ISIS fighters and were able to bring in air power. This often happened when ISIS had repurposed the interior of a building into a fighting position or a machine-gun nest. We couldn't destroy it beforehand because it was not easily identifiable from the air. And everything would stop when the Iraqi military stumbled onto it. Bad for our teammates, but good for us. These were easy targets and got the strike cell in the fight, which was becoming less commonplace. Instead of participating, we started to find ourselves as spectators, enjoying the war from our cozy little air-conditioned room.

I had expected to watch a battle like I was at the movie theater. We had the cameras and the time. I wanted to see the heroics of the tactical fight as Iraqi security forces outmaneuvered ISIS, the drama of the struggle, and the emotional toll of the loss. I wanted to be entertained in my high castle, safely observing the battle and getting involved when it suited us. But this isn't how a campaign works. Instead, it was dreadfully slow. Hours of watching people stand around, doing nothing. There would be an occasional advance followed by a long halt. City blocks were recaptured one at a time. Eventually, the black flag came down, replaced by an Iraqi one. But the fighting was far from over.

I acknowledge that it was a brutal fight, and many Iraqi military members should be celebrated for their bravery and sacrifice. Battles filled with heroes who went above beyond the call of duty. But not in this book. I found most of June incredibly dull.

I wasn't very interested in the Fallujah campaign, at least not until the epic last day. This is mainly because I wasn't part of the fight. I think most of us are selfish, viewing the world through our own personal endeavors. I couldn't shoot HIMARS during the operation, so it was hard to care. The city was over 100 kilometers from where my launchers were located, well past the maximum range of the rockets. No matter how much I wanted to move them into a better position, it wasn't that type of war. We sat idle for most of June. I had a few missions here and there in areas we had already liberated, destroying several suspicious vehicles and knocking over an abandoned artillery piece, which we declared neutralized. Still, all around, it was a slow month.

However, the campaign took a unique turn one evening at the end of June. We noticed ISIS was starting to stage vehicles for some sort of convoy. We got some drones overhead and started working on the strike-approval process. Nothing out of the ordinary. But then, more vehicles began getting in line. And then more. Something strange was clearly happening, and we let it develop for a couple of hours to better understand the situation. By nightfall, there were over a hundred vehicles parked in lines, and people were loading bags into them throughout. After a hard-fought month, the remnants of ISIS in central Iraq were leaving Fallujah.

It was an easier battle than we expected. It was a full-on retreat. It was also the perfect target.

We all started brainstorming how to destroy as many vehicles as possible and let the fewest people escape. However, we were pretty limited in our available resources, with only a few bombs and Hellfire missiles available and the target out of range of rocket artillery. None of the plans would work well, but it would still be quite the show. We settled on an attack method and briefed our approach.

But our request was denied. That was a surprise. A strike was rarely denied. Not only that, but we were also told to stand down. It wasn't just that our solution wasn't approved; the mission as a whole was denied. We argued our case but lost. We weren't going to strike them at all.

It was so anti-climactic to just let them leave. This was not how we expected to win. I went to bed frustrated that night. We had missed an excellent opportunity to remove ISIS fighters and equipment from the broader battlefield. But a new day held new opportunities.

I walked into the strike cell the following morning carrying my usual feast. It's easy to complain about military life, but they do feed you well.

"What the hell?" I said aloud, shocked to find the room overflowing with senior leaders and mid-grade officers I had never seen before. It looked like everyone on the base had gathered in our quaint little room, and the senior visitors were a little too comfortable sitting in the open seats they found. I wasn't about to let that stand, rank be damned.

"Sorry, sir, but I need that seat," I said very politely to a colonel who had commandeered my spot in the third row. "I need my workstation to knock out my morning reports right away." This was a lie; I didn't write any reports, and I had nothing to do. But I wanted to eat. I think he knew that. He looked disgruntled to have to stand and be moved to the side of the room by a lowly captain. But he was in no position to argue. Visitors didn't get seats, so he moved with no greater complaint than a frowny face.

"Just in time," the strike director said with a huge grin as I looked around, confused.

The ISIS convoy was still there and had continued growing. People were loading into the vehicles and getting ready to hit the road. Nine of our televisions were focused on the vehicles. I didn't notice at first, but they were all different feeds with different angles.

We had an arsenal in the sky. "In time for what? Did somebody change their mind? Are we striking the convoy?" I wondered if a convincing argument had reached the ears of the decision makers. While expelling ISIS from central Iraq was our mission, them moving back to Syria or up north to Mosul was not the win we wanted. That just shifted the problem to someone else's area of operations. This was a chance to take a piece off the board entirely. Leadership agreed. It was going to be a good morning.

Overnight, the senior leaders coordinated the repurposing of strike assets across the Central Command theater. I arrived just in time for the A-10 Warthog attack aircraft operating in Syria to check on station over Fallujah. The A-10 is the ultimate close-air-support aircraft. It can fly low and slow relative to other fixed-wing strike aircraft, giving it the best chance to successfully engage multiple targets on the ground. Additionally, it has a 30-millimeter Gatling gun in its nose that can fire nearly four thousand rounds per minute, roughly thirty rounds every second. The infamous "brrrt" from the gun signifies death for any in its path. The rounds can pierce armored military vehicles; they would make short work of these random civilian cars and trucks. We would obliterate the convoy, and it would be a hell of a show.

It's a strange thing watching a battle unfold via drone feed. We couldn't see the aircraft. Instead, our eyes focused on the target area, leveraging numerous angles to get a broad perspective. There was also no sound. I have mentioned this before, but it stood out during this strike. Sound is critical for appreciating war's violence and a munition's destructive impact. Still, everyone was on their feet as the gun run began, prepared to observe the once-in-a-lifetime event.

Even though we knew it was beginning, the explosions were still sudden and unexpected. Unlike our usual strikes, there was no moment just before the impact where we could see the rocket or bomb. The guns on the A-10s began firing and vehicles started exploding everywhere. It was drastically different from our standard missions. Instead of one or two large explosions, there were hundreds of small explosions as the powerful aircraft spit 30 rounds a second into the convoy. Because the depleted uranium rounds passed right through vehicles, and the passengers, the explosions appeared to be coming from underneath the vehicles as the rounds made contact with the road's surface. It was a strange site, almost like the convoy had been parked on a minefield that suddenly activated.

It was beautiful. The strike cell erupted in cheers, curses at the enemy, and laughter. This was how the war was supposed to end, with fire and destruction. This strike was the decisive battle, eradicating the plague from central Iraq. I was proud to have been a part of it.

It all happened so fast. Few vehicles could get out of the convoy line, and a second gun run sealed the fate of anyone still inside a vehicle. ISIS fighters scrambled in every direction, fleeing for their lives. It was supposed to be their Exodus, their mass movement from Fallujah. Instead, it was their Armageddon. The A-10s did their job; the convoy was no more. Then it was our turn.

Our televisions shifted from the wreckage to the stragglers. We had numerous armed drones and fighter aircraft flying overhead, prepared to exploit the chaos and confusion and hunt down anyone fleeing the scene. We knew we couldn't get everyone, so we focused on groups, raining down Hellfires and dropping bombs where we could get the most damage per munition.

It was so easy. Running out of ammunition didn't take long, and most of the aircraft eventually needed to leave to refuel. The mission was over, and we proceeded to assess the wreckage.

It felt like a scene from a movie. Over one hundred vehicles were shredded, burned, and in pieces. It reminded me of the highway of death from the First Gulf War. There were bodies sprawled on the ground in every direction, with no rhyme or reason as to where they were fleeing before being gunned down. It was a complete and total victory. There were no tallying-up results during this battle-damage assessment; there was too much carnage. We killed them by the hundreds that morning.

The adrenaline of the strike gradually wore off, but the mood didn't change. Joy. Awe. We hated them and were ecstatic we had accomplished our mission. I still feel that way. Is that wrong? I don't look back at this moment with regret or sorrow. It does not haunt me like some more personal strikes. I didn't empathize with this force of evil. As I said before, they deserved to die. They were not our peers or counterparts who were victims of different circumstances. They were simply ISIS that day. The enemy. Evil. And we exterminated them, decisively ending our part of the war.

CHAPTER 22

The Iraqi Tea Party

It's the little things.

With ISIS expelled from Fallujah, central Iraq was effectively liberated—a term I struggle with when I think of the destructive cost associated with that success. With this victory came an instant reduction in required coalition support to the Iraqi military in our area of operations. My role had diminished overnight, and our mission was no longer the main effort. Instead, the coalition began transitioning to the next phase of the operation; the priority shifted north to Mosul. This next phase would become a long and hard fight, overshadowing what we had accomplished in central Iraq. While this didn't mean everyone got to just pack up and go home, it did allow me to do just that.

Back home, my pregnant wife was pretty far along with our second child, and I was determined not to miss the birth. While I have missed many life events because of my choice to serve in the military, the birth of a child is one you can never make up. At the same time, the coalition's shift to the north meant my day-to-day life had become rather dull and my desire to sit in Iraq twiddling my thumbs was decreasing rapidly. This combination of reduced mission requirements and my family situation at home justified my request for early redeployment.

Because my commander back in the United States was not my biggest fan, I was surprised this request was approved. Shortly after raising the issue, my leadership decided to bring a new HIMARS liaison officer to Union III and send me home. My replacement didn't come from the group already deployed to Iraq, which was a strange decision in my eyes. At this point in the deployment, numerous lieutenants had served at the firing point with the launchers. They were intimately familiar with the mission and the nuances of processing fire missions in our fancy field-artillery computer. Instead, the decision was made to deploy a senior lieutenant who was still back home. I experienced this game on my first deployment, with random lieutenants deploying late to Iraq to ensure as many people as possible got the invaluable deployment opportunity, and the credibility that came alongside a combat patch on their shoulder. It was often frustrating to deal with.

However, my concern about my replacement's lack of mission knowledge was quickly put to rest. After receiving her orders, she reached out via e-mail, excited about the opportunity. She had stayed abreast of our operations in Iraq and was ready to hit the books and build up her fire-mission processing skills. As the rest of us had discovered when we first deployed, though, the books in question—Army doctrine—had not caught up to how we operated in Iraq. Instead, I bombarded her with our lessons learned and anything else I could think of to share so she could do some preparation before arriving.

When she finally arrived, I was able to spend a couple of days with her before I had to leave. I needed to ensure she could learn from my mistakes and be ready to build on the lessons we had learned so far. Even though the position responsibilities were diminishing, it was still challenging to navigate, and her rank wouldn't make managing necessary relationships any easier. Although, to be fair, I may be abrasive at times, so some of those challenges might have been on me.

The focus of the handoff was fire-mission processing. Everything else could be learned on the job if required, not to mention that my noncommissioned officer was staying on board with her to finish the deployment, so he could address the technical challenges I couldn't teach her even if I wanted to.

In the short time we had together, we worked through our operating procedures and the fire-mission processes as much as possible. Adding the necessary realism to the training required us to conduct a couple of actual missions together as a culminating event. However, as already noted, strike-cell operations had slowed down dramatically.

We only identified a couple of targets during our handoff, few of which were appropriate or even feasible for HIMARS. When a potential mission did arise, I leveraged the need to qualify my replacement as a sell for HIMARS, angering the Air Force officers who were just as bored as I was and wanted to get back in the fight. This worked a few times and we got her some experience under supervision (which it turned out she didn't need much of).

The first mission we fired together was simple. The team identified a large warehouse that needed to be destroyed. No enemy fighters were inside the building, so it was not a timely issue. However, when we started working up a proposed solution, it quickly became apparent HIMARS was not the best asset for the mission. In fact, far from it. The building's size meant we would have to fire numerous rockets. But there was no objection on my end; it was a great stat-builder mission before heading home. Realistically, a 2,000-pound bomb dropped from an aircraft would have been the best response. I knew it. The air-liaison officer knew it. Even the director knew it.

But this target was an easy opportunity for "Team HIMARS" to work through the entire mission process as slowly as needed, blooding the new team member. The mission was successful but unimportant. We did enough damage to call it a win and got through the first-mission jitters with a low-visibility strike. With that accomplished, the last item on my checklist was to help get her a kill. Dark, right?

The next mission was dynamic. We had to move quickly or lose an opportunity. This was a more realistic test to validate our handoff and to put strike-cell operations into perspective for her.

"Sir, one of the drone operators is reporting sniper fire. Getting the feed up on screen six and dropping the coordinates into the group chat time now," the battle captain reported.

The feed from the unarmed drone came through and we identified an ISIS fighter lying on a blanket in an alleyway between numerous buildings, wielding an enormous weapon that had to be some sort of sniper rifle. Some local Iraqi military members were in trouble if he was half-decent at firing it.

"There are no friendlies in the area," the director replied. "Let's figure out what he's shooting at and start coming up with some options. The target is the rifle; the fighter is a bonus. I want that thing off the battlefield."

We watched him closely as we began working up strike options. He was firing the weapon at something, so we followed the path of his barrel and eventually found his partner. We deduced the partner was assisting the shooter by offering corrections and adjustments for a practice target we couldn't identify.

They were training.

While our game may have ended a couple weeks prior, I still casually joked that playing with guns was not authorized in Iraq. But, all kidding aside, this was not a good sign for Iraqi forces in the area. Even if central Iraq was no longer the battleground it had been a few months prior, a sniper team could cause significant damage to an unsuspecting military force.

A Hellfire missile would have made the most sense for the strike. It was the fastest response option and had the smallest blast radius, limiting any collateral damage. However, a Hellfire wasn't available at the time. The sniper rifle needed to be destroyed, and the opportunity to strike was fleeting. So, we scrambled to pitch a couple of solutions. But, as we looked at options, we realized this mission was going to be a low-collateral-damage challenge, even for HIMARS. On the plus side, that meant dropping a bomb from an aircraft wasn't a viable option.

Because the blanket in the alleyway was between two buildings, we struggled to create a solution that allowed us to avoid unnecessary infrastructure damage. This was one of those moments when a suboptimal solution was better than not engaging at all. Generally speaking, a point-detonation or proximity fuze is the best option for troops in the open, often against more than one enemy fighter because it's an expensive rocket, and we tried to always get the best bang for our buck. But those fuzes wouldn't work in this situation because of the collateral-damage estimates.

After my replacement and I spent some time in the second row with our targeting officer, I finally spoke up: "Sir, our best bet is a single rocket, delay fuze." We crafted the weaponeering solution as a workaround for potential collateral-damage issues.

It was going to be a weird mission.

"Will that work?" the director asked. "Delaying the rocket on a person."

"It's not preferred, but it will do the job. To be honest, it will probably be pretty horrific on the receiving end, but this guy's going to have a bad day no matter how we fuze the rocket," I replied. That got a few laughs.

While this was not the most conventional approach, it met the intent of destroying the sniper rifle. Theoretically, the rocket would pass through the blanket the sniper was sitting on—presumably killing the shooter in the process—and then explode after the rocket's velocity drove it roughly one meter into the ground. We mentally braced ourselves for a pretty horrific scene.

Our airspace manager had been working on deconfliction measures while the rest of us debated weaponeering options. Once decided, we quickly moved the launchers to the firing point and requested final approval. However, before we finished this conversation, the other enemy fighter who was acting as a spotter started moving, heading back toward the partner with the sniper rifle.

"Stand by!" the director hollered. "Target might be moving."

We froze, waiting to see if the opportunity was lost. Because of the flight time of the rocket, it didn't make sense to shoot and hope they were slow packers. We were prepared to follow that rifle with our drone if they packed up and left; we would strike them wherever they settled next. Instead, when the two men linked up at the blanket, the spotter got down and started working with the gun.

"Ha! It looks like the spotter is making corrections," the director added. "Let's get them both while we can. The target remains valid. You're approved to strike."

My replacement relayed the commands to the launchers and, when they replied, she took over the strike cell with a confident yell: "Shot, all rockets fired!"

With operations as slow as they were, the mission was the best show in town, and the team was itching for a good strike. We had everyone's undivided attention.

Without warning, the enemy fighters began packing everything up. "Shit!" I yelled. "They're closing up shop, looks like sniper training is over."

Realizing he should have shot sooner, the director looked to me for an update: "How long until the rocket's impact?"

A while. The mission was near the rocket's maximum range. Before launch, we calculated a flight time of almost three minutes. "Just over a minute, sir," my replacement replied, taking ownership of the mission. "It's going to be close."

As she broke the bad news, it became clear this rocket would probably not arrive in time if they were leaving. Waiting to engage when we noticed the spotter moving appeared to be an expensive mistake. But there was no calling the rocket back; it was on a collision course. Both men were standing, packing their gear into a surprisingly large bag and disassembling the rifle for easier transport.

As usual, we offered them some strong encouragement to stick around for another minute, hollering at the television, willing the mission to work out with some more of my inappropriate language and drawing some negative attention from the director.

And it worked.

Not really. But they stayed. Once their equipment was packed, they stopped and started unloading a much smaller bag. It wasn't clear initially what they were doing, but the pieces quickly came together.

"They're having a tea party!" someone yelled. They were going to take a tea break before returning to wherever they came from. We couldn't help but laugh, jesting about the "worst picnic ever," and the "tea party from hell." They sat down and took in the moment, enjoying their hard-earned break. We interrupted the party ... "I guess picnics aren't allowed in Iraq."

The rocket blasted right through the center of the blanket, traveling so fast the two enemy fighters had no time to react. The explosion was weird, almost muted, as the rocket attempted to burrow into the ground. The alleyway filled with smoke and dust before we could observe what had happened, forcing us to wait for the official assessment; but we all knew the mission was successful; nobody could survive a blast like that.

When the smoke cleared, there was nothing to assess. I'm sure it would have been much worse if our feed was in color. Those surrounding buildings were probably painted with the remnants of those two men.

"Vaporized," someone said. We all had a good laugh at the comment, joking about a pretty horrific impact. Spirits were high; we were happy to return to the fight.

I'm not sure exactly what happened, but we called it a success. The sniper rifle was destroyed, and its operators were dead. I doubt there was much anyone would recover from the scene. These men wouldn't receive a burial when all was said and done. They simply vanished from existence.

We laughed at the tea-party incident for my last few days in Iraq. Is it wrong to feel this way and still laugh about it as I recount these events? While some stories are hard to tell or even think about, this one still makes me smile, but not because people died. I don't laugh at their expense or devalue their lives. It took me some time and reflection to realize this, accepting that laughing is okay. Instead, these were such strange circumstances that it was funny how life sometimes works out, the coin-flip decision that may cost someone their life, and the ridiculous effects of the rocket.

That may be wrong. I don't know. But I no longer care.

I feel good about this mission. We likely saved more lives than we took. I have accepted that I can have fond memories of horrible things. And I know I wasn't the only one in the strike cell laughing throughout the mission. I also doubt I'm the only one who still tells this story and smirks, reminded how strange it was to put a delayed round through those men, obliterating them like we cast a meteor down from the sky. Maybe I just look at this mission fondly because it was my last. Regardless, shortly after the infamous Iraqi Tea Party, I headed home to reintegrate into everyday life, to wake up from the weird dream that was my third military deployment.

CHAPTER 23

And a Wake Up

It's not something I can just forget and move on from; it's part of who I am now.

Mission complete. We successfully expelled ISIS from central Iraq, and the coalition effort shifted to the north. A new HIMARS firing point was created, and they even had their own rocket-artillery liaison officer ready to take a similar journey to mine. Just as it was my responsibility to ensure my replacement was competent, it was my duty to help the new HIMARS liaison up north as much as possible. I partnered with him shortly after he assumed his responsibilities at our northern strike cell in Erbil. I highlighted the challenges I had faced when coordinating rocket artillery and shared the tactics, techniques, and procedures we developed throughout my deployment.

At the same time, my replacement had demonstrated she was ready to assume the duties of the HIMARS liaison officer in central Iraq, minimal as they were with the shift in priorities. In fact, right after the tea-party mission, she took that seat in the back row next to the director, prepared to take charge. I lost my seat and with it my role in the strike cell. I felt comfortable hanging up my hat.

My fight was over.

One afternoon, it became official. I stood before the strike cell to receive my end-of-tour award before getting on a helicopter back to Baghdad International Airport that evening. I was surprisingly excited about the award because it was a new one to add to the dress uniform, a joint award. I laugh at how accurate the famous quote from

Napoleon Bonaparte is: "A soldier will fight long and hard for a bit of colored ribbon."

I listened intently, standing proud as the general listed my statistics, highlighting my contribution to the fight. The deployment had come full circle. I was the one with the data sheet and the impressive combat statistics. The new team members that had been trickling in looked on, likely wondering if they would have a chance to achieve similar results or if they had missed the war.

I was proud of my role in the conflict and had done my part. Over the course of seven months, I fired 504 rockets, killing 609 ISIS fighters and destroying countless buildings and vehicles.

I also contributed in less tangible ways, helping to shape rocket-artillery policy in Iraq and Syria and developing employment techniques that dramatically decreased fire-mission processing time, making us faster and more responsive to the maneuver forces on the ground. However, you will not find those qualitative statistics in an evaluation or an award. While these contributions were important for supporting the Iraqi military, they have broader implications for the employment of US rocket artillery in a future conflict. I have continued exploring this topic as my career has progressed.

After the general pinned the award on my chest, he told those in attendance the story of our first meeting. I didn't realize I had made an impression but, apparently, my motivation had created some memorable moments for those around me. During his first week in Iraq, he observed several missions. The one that stood out, the one he said he would never forget, was a HIMARS mission. He recounted being caught off guard by the intense captain in the strike cell screaming about zombies and using less-than-appropriate language. Everyone laughed as they also remembered a handful of my outbursts and sometimes over-the-top intensity.

I was surprised how hard it was to say goodbye. This was my first time leaving a deployment by myself. It was a strange feeling. I wanted to go home, but I also felt like I was quitting the team and leaving my friends to complete the mission without me. It's weird how close you can get to people in such a short time in these conditions, sharing hardships and unique experiences. There was no escaping them. Like them or not, the people around you are all you have on a deployment. As I left, I received what has become one of my favorite military mementos, a t-shirt that reads, "ISIS EXTERMINATION TOUR." And then I was on my way. It was time to go home. It was time to wake up.

Seven months "and a wake up." After three deployments, I was very familiar with this military saying. It's often just a way of counting down to mission completion:

"How much time do you have left?"

"Six weeks and a wake up."

But it carries a deeper meaning for those individuals processing this chapter of their life, those reinserting themselves into the world they left behind. The basic idea is that the deployment is a dream, an event you can slog through knowing it will abruptly end. This allows someone to suddenly move on, letting the experience become some hazy memory.

But that's not how it happens. The world doesn't freeze in place while the service member is deployed, no matter how much it feels like it should. In fact, everything changes. Small things only change a little, but other aspects are unrecognizable from what they once were. I encourage soldiers to read Joe Haldeman's *The Forever War* before their first time experiencing the shock of coming home from a deployment. Haldeman, a Vietnam War veteran, thrusts his protagonist into exaggerated and absurd circumstances on each return trip home from war where the world has fundamentally changed, like money no longer being necessary or all human reproduction being conducted in laboratories.

While it's rarely the case that the world changes so drastically while we are away, at the individual level, it often feels like it did. This can be dramatic adjustments to someone's life situation, like a death in the family, a divorce, or even a child born while they were away. But changes can also seem minor to everyone except the person reintegrating.

I remember coming home from my first deployment after my wife had moved us to an apartment in the neighboring city. It wasn't a surprise and didn't seem like a big deal initially. However, everything compounded around this. I didn't know my address, zip code, how to get home, how to get back to work from the new place, which drawer had the silverware, or anything else that went along with moving. While this is common for anyone when they move, it was different for me because the household was already settled. I was an outsider and felt uncomfortable in my own home. But it passes and, eventually, you reach a new normal.

I have become more accustomed to this reintegration process over the years. But it's still strange. After seven long months of staring at those screens and watching people die all day, I was excited to come home. I was ready to put the events behind me. Since I traveled as an individual, there was no big welcome party, no fire trucks spraying arches for the plane when it taxied, and no gaggle of older veteran volunteers to share stories with. Just me getting off the plane as if I had been gone on some routine travel.

Except the family that met me when I returned had changed ... everything changes. My wife was seven months pregnant, and my son had grown dramatically, not just in size, but also in how well he could communicate. They had continued living while I was gone; I had missed an essential part of both of their lives.

The real reintegration began when the excitement of being back in the United States wore off. People only care about what you did or where you were for the first couple of days after returning. Then it's back to normalcy, forced onto you before most are ready. Regardless of support systems, it's a hard transition and you can't help but feel like you are doing it alone. Everyone has routines established, and you are inserting yourself into them, a difficult and often awkward endeavor.

And then there was the boredom. There is a scene from the movie *The Hurt Locker* that has always stuck with me. Having just returned home from a ridiculously exaggerated combat deployment, the main character finds himself standing in the cereal aisle at the grocery store, unable to make a selection. He was thrust into everyday life and found he had traded the meaning and purpose he had in the war for the monotony of civil society. In doing so, he lost himself.

I am sad to admit how much I have related to that moment in the cereal aisle.

After being home for a few weeks, I returned to work and shared my experiences with anyone who would listen. Eventually, once I ran out of stories to tell or people interested in listening to them, I went on with life as if the deployment never happened. Like the main character in *The Hurt Locker*, I volunteered to return to Iraq to finish the mission. In about nine months, our sister battalion was deploying for a similar adventure to support efforts in northern Iraq, and I asked to join them. But that's not how it works; my request was denied. Life is not a movie.

This was for the best. I didn't actually want to go back. I hate Iraq. I hate the Iraqi military. I hate being deployed and away from my family. And it wasn't a cause I cared about, not anymore. But in the military it feels like it's what we're supposed to do, what all paths lead to. Deployments aren't some surprise or penalty; they are literally what most of us signed up for.

I didn't get to deploy again to finish off ISIS. Instead, I was asked to help prepare our sister battalion, to identify what we learned during our trip and ensure they knew our tactics, techniques, and procedures. I was back in the fight for a few weeks. But that, too, was fleeting.

I moved on. My war was over again. For real this time. Unable to be directly involved in the fight against ISIS, I watched the rest of the war unfold from afar, excited to see the final phase and read about the role HIMARS would play in it. I needed closure; I needed our missions to have meaning in the grand campaign to exterminate ISIS.

The Iraqi military began its final push against ISIS not long after I returned home, and the battle for Mosul that ensued was like nothing my team had experienced. The operation was immense, overshadowing our efforts in the war. Central Iraq seemed like the North Africa campaign in World War II, while Mosul was D-Day. Our operations may have been essential to the war on many levels, but few will remember the Hit Campaign or the Fallujah exodus. However, these actions set up the engagement in Mosul, isolating ISIS in a final stronghold.

ISIS was an animal trapped in a corner. There was no option but to fight. The challenges of the Ramadi campaign resurfaced. To liberate Mosul and stomp out ISIS in Iraq, the coalition resorted to heavy bombardments wherever the Iraqi military met resistance. The battle lasted for months. It was brutal urban warfare fought one neighborhood at a time. Thousands of ISIS fighters and Iraqi military members were killed or wounded in the operation. Additionally, because of the inherent risk to civilians in this type of fight, thousands of noncombatants were also killed, and nearly a million were displaced.

In the summer of 2017, Mosul was liberated. By the end of the year, the Iraqi Government declared ISIS was defeated in Iraq. Still, when it was all said and done, what we had foreshadowed in our early offensives had come to fruition. To free the nation and expel the cancer in its cities, we had to destroy it. Mosul, like Ramadi, was turned into rubble. No more black flags fly in Iraq, but the nation is on the verge of becoming a failed state.

The Middle East will undoubtedly draw our attention again in the future. However, as I believed in 2011, that will be someone else's problem, a war for the next generation.

A new patch on my sleeve, two new ribbons on my dress uniform, an awesome T-shirt that no longer fits, and some fuzzy memories. A strange dream that I had finally woken up from. That is all the deployment became to me after enough time. Although I knew I wasn't going back, I had to keep training. I'd spent my entire time in the HIMARS battalion away from the actual launchers. It was time to get back to training artillery soldiers, back in the dirt and away from the little secure room where I had fought the war. The next part of my journey would be a return to my youth, to when I first joined the Army as a bright-eyed junior officer excited to make things go boom.

CHAPTER 24

Taking the Guidon

It just wasn't the same. I knew what the real thing felt like; I couldn't pretend anymore.

As much as I was excited to return to America, I wasn't too hopeful about my future in the Army. I worked for a man who didn't like me. In all fairness, I didn't like him either. But in a strict hierarchal structure, this disadvantaged me considerably. If he wanted, he could ruin my career; sometimes, it felt like that was the path we were headed down together. So, when an opportunity to leave his organization presented itself, I took it. My brigade commander—my boss's boss's boss—was proud of how well the Iraq mission had gone and had read my airspace article. He offered me a job as the commander of the brigade headquarters element, an escape that undoubtedly saved my career.

It wasn't glamorous, but it was a command. I took the guidon, the flag of an organization that serves as a symbol of responsibility, advancing me to the next phase of my military career. I became an administrator, coordinating fitness tests, rifle ranges, drug tests, and an assortment of mandatory PowerPoint briefs that seemed to consume most of our training time. My calendar filled up with all the additional tasks associated with property management, mandatory briefings, and discipline issues. I went from killing people to paperwork in the blink of an eye.

I got back into the fight a year later. Kind of. I got to go pretend again. People don't stay in positions long in the Army. It's not because they are good or bad at their jobs; it's just the nature of the system. So, after the leadership from my old battalion finally left, I petitioned to take over a HIMARS battery and return to the unit I had gone to war with.

Less than a week after taking the second guidon, I found myself in the field leading artillery men and women in some outlandish notional fight that was nothing like the war I had just served in. Instead, most of our training was spent driving around, covering vast distances with our launchers, and dealing with random enemy forces sneaking into our area. It was fun, but it wasn't what I expected, not after all the lessons we had just learned overseas about the challenges of airspace deconfliction and the nuances of fire-mission processing.

I played the game, but I did it my way. I threw out the book and fought in a way that made sense to the situation at hand, a way to address the problem we were actually facing. This didn't go over well with many people, but the unit performed well enough, so I didn't get in too much trouble for going off script.

After a week or so of our simulated war, we transitioned to shooting the launchers—albeit with reduced-range practice rockets. It was funny, I had processed the fire missions for hundreds of rockets in training and combat, but I hadn't physically been down to fire the mission with the launchers since I was a cadet conducting my first fire mission 10 years prior. Just like it was then, I was the new guy. Most of the soldiers in the battery knew me from the deployment, but it was still my first mission with the team; soldiers love playing jokes on the new guy.

The sun was setting at the Orchard Combat Training Center in Idaho when we got everything set for our first fire mission with me as the commander. I took a moment to appreciate the experience, to take in the reds and pinks of the desert sky as the sun crested the horizon, to smell the open air away from the chaos of the city, and to embrace the silence from my isolated vantage point. My first sergeant and I could see for miles in every direction from our little hilltop where we watched the launchers, the two of us lounging on the vehicle's hood. But our eyes were fixated on the first crew, nervous that something would go wrong and anxious to start the process.

"You ready for this, sir? You excited to finally see them in action?" my first sergeant asked.

"I told you, it's not my first time," I replied.

"I don't care how many times I see it, this shit always pumps me up!" he added. He loved what he did. After 20 years, he was still giddy to start blowing stuff up. "Besides, this one's special ... trust me," he said with a big grin.

I should have known something was up by the way he said it.

The rocket fired, and the sound ripped through the air a second later, a thunderous roar that I felt deep in my core. There was a sudden boom that would have rattled our windows if they weren't just plastic squares with zippers. I had forgotten how loud the rocket's initial ignition explosion was, and it nearly made me fall off the hood of the truck.

I had fired hundreds of rockets, but I lived in a weird, muted world when I was in Iraq. I had forgotten the sounds of the battlefield. It never takes long to realize that combat stinks. That evening reminded me combat is also loud, and not everyone is privileged to sit in a little air-conditioned office away from the carnage.

We watched the crew fire a few more rockets to complete their qualification. After they were complete, someone left the launcher and started picking things up from the fire area. Shortly after, I heard some chatter on the radio in the background that sounded like laughter. I dismissed it and went back to observing the missions. But they were different than I remembered. I wasn't enthralled by the boom. I don't know if seeing the destruction on the other side of the missions changed my perspective, but the excitement had faded.

I didn't find out why that first mission was special until later that evening. We had been geared up for battle during the training: body armor, helmets, and all the associated knickknacks. But once all the firing was complete, we had the opportunity to get comfortable, and the joke became obvious. At some point in the day, while my first sergeant kept me distracted, some soldiers in the battery had dug around in my bag and taken my two hats, the only ones I had packed with me. Afterward, my hats mysteriously ended up taped to the back of a launcher. Needless to say, they were utterly obliterated. So, while everyone else got to take off their helmets and get comfortable, I had to keep mine on. For those unaware, being outside without something on your head is a severe no-no in the Army, worse even than being caught with your hands in your pockets.

When we formed up outside, I stood out like a sore thumb as I came to the front of the unit to congratulate everyone on their hard work in Idaho. Of the roughly eighty of us standing in the field that evening, only one was still wearing their helmet. Nearly ten years after my awkward waddle to a launcher for my first mission, I once again looked ridiculous in front of the soldiers. But this experience was more endearing.

The soldiers got a kick out of the moment and the launcher crew who had destroyed my hats presented me the remnants: a tattered bit of camouflage cloth and a piece of rim. It was hardly recognizable as ever being a hat after what the rocket's backblast had done to it. I wasn't mad, though. It's an easy tradition to maintain. I was part of the unit, back to being a regular soldier. I belonged somewhere. And I was surprised to realize how important this was for me.

I moved on from my experience in the war and focused on preparing for the next one. I was determined to train my unit for the inevitable return to the Middle East, avoiding the status-quo approach of training for the war we were most comfortable with. However, I quickly learned I had little authority in my unit's training. Training objectives are prescribed, and I found myself racing to achieve each required wicket and then starting the process over again. At a minimum, I ensured that actual HIMARS training always included multiple precision-aimpoint missions, a fundamental task all rocket artillerymen needed to become intimately familiar with.

However, there was one hurdle preventing me from moving on completely: more accurately, one wheelbarrow. After accepting the new normalcy of my life, I was reminded that some memories are stronger than others. I discovered that some experiences stick with you, no matter how much time has passed, shaping how you view the world. An incident mentally put me back in Iraq and forced me to take a holistic look at warfare and my role in it, a catalyst for reflection that stays with me as a constant reminder of my actions.

CHAPTER 25

To Walk a Mile

*I still go there at night sometimes. But it's different now;
it changes as I get older. I fear what it will become.*

I don't often think about any of my time overseas, but writing this memoir has unearthed a lot of powerful memories. My time abroad provided experiences that undoubtedly shaped me as a military officer and played a significant part in my development as a man. Most of the time, however, the experience is relegated to distant memories, a fever dream that is best not to dwell on. In fact, the only time a deployment comes to mind is when I'm talking with a fellow service member, swapping stories and playing the small-world game where I try to figure out if I've been to the same place or worked with the same people as someone I just met. But generally, these memories have faded. They're still a part of me, but not defining me.

This is not the case for everyone. I have friends who became hyper-vigilant drivers after dealing with improvised explosive devices, some who developed a violent hatred for people of Middle Eastern descent, others who grew disenfranchised with our government because of what they had to do abroad, and, sadly, a handful who have taken their own lives. For most of us, though, a deployment was just a thing we did, no different than other military experiences. For me, there has only been one time when these memories crept back to the forefront of my mind, a powerful memory that overwhelmed me and made me reassess what warfare meant to me. A memory that has stuck with me since.

I had been home from the deployment for roughly two years, long enough that life was normal again, and killing ISIS was a distant memory. I successfully reintegrated into the household and was comfortable in the workplace. Then, on a chilly autumn day in Washington, we took a trip to the pumpkin patch, and everything from the deployment came flooding back.

The pumpkin patch was a family tradition we had put off for a few years because of work requirements. It's always a fun day for the kids and our standard method for purchasing Halloween pumpkins. I was having a great time watching my oldest son just be a little person let loose into the wild, free and happy. The youngest was experiencing the tradition for the first time.

After we enjoyed all the fun events that creative people can concoct using pumpkins and hay, we transitioned to pumpkin picking. At one point, my wife, stubborn as she is, took over pushing the wheelbarrow we would use to haul our selected pumpkins. At the same time, my little men ran around examining the merchandise, finding us the best pumpkin in the patch. At first, I simply watched, smiling. I was glad to be back with my family and content to merely appreciate the calm, making a deliberate effort to just be in the now and enjoy the moment. And then, suddenly, it became one of the worst days of my life. I had a panic attack.

I was suddenly hot, burning up and uncomfortable in an unfamiliar way. I ripped off my sweatshirt, overreacting to the sudden shift in temperature. But it was more than simply overheating. My heart was beating rapidly, racing; I felt like it was going to burst out of my chest. I tried to calm myself, taking slow breaths, but my body didn't cooperate. Panic washed over me, and I squeezed my eyes shut, attempting to figure out what was happening and trying to escape for a moment.

That made everything worse. Much worse.

There was no darkness when I closed my eyes. Instead, my imagination took over, consuming my reality. We were no longer gathering our Halloween pumpkins; no one was. I was still in the field, but it was different; it was darker and soundless. We were in a drone feed. I looked at the wheelbarrows around me, horrified to see they were hauling corpses. I couldn't make out an individual, just limbs dangling over the side, lifeless. It was a scene I remembered vividly from a mission, but it was somehow superimposed onto my reality back home. I didn't know what to do.

I opened my eyes, breathing heavily. I wandered around for a minute, looking into other people's wheelbarrows. It sounds crazy, but I needed to ensure it was just a short memory, a haunting daydream, and nothing more. I received some confused looks as I invaded personal bubbles, but I didn't care. In my panic, I lost track of my family. After a few moments, I spotted my wife walking down a path, pushing our wheelbarrow, her back to me.

Unwanted visions dominated my mind. I couldn't help but imagine her cleaning up the battlefield, toddler beside her. I thought of legs dangling from her wheelbarrow. A stranger's? Mine? She remained firm, unfazed by her battlefield responsibility, a military spouse trained and prepared to lose their loved one. This was a burden I had forced on her.

It was a ridiculous thought.

And yet, I couldn't shake it. I knew nothing was in that wheelbarrow except maybe a pumpkin they had picked without me, but it didn't matter. My mind was playing tricks on me. My feelings weren't rational, and I was overwhelmed by a wave of powerful emotions I didn't understand.

The only answer was to leave. I grabbed my wife and told her as much. We needed to abandon the wheelbarrow; we could get pumpkins another day. I was panicking and needed to get out of that field to calm down, regain my composure, and assess what had just happened. She didn't understand, and the little ones were not ready to leave. I was ruining our fall adventure for no tangible reason.

I was being silly. There was nothing actually wrong. I couldn't explain it to her. I still can't. To be perfectly honest, I'm not sure I fully understand what happened. All I knew then was that I needed to leave, whether they were ready or not. Of course, they came with me, and I was glad about it because, at that moment, I didn't want to be alone.

The car ride home was uncomfortable. I wanted to share my feelings but couldn't show her that weakness. Would she think less of me? What I was feeling didn't make sense to me. How could I expect it to make sense to someone else? I knew she wanted to know, to understand and support me, but neither of us was ready for the conversation. I still struggle to talk about it; it's unsettling.

So, it didn't happen. I wouldn't burden her that day, nor any other, choosing to work through the moment alone. We both remember it as the wheelbarrow incident, but I don't think I ever really helped her understand what happened at the pumpkin patch or what it meant to me. I'm not sure I ever will. Writing has provided the only real opportunity to explore that day and reflect, to share the moment with my family.

In the days that followed, I wrestled with that moment. I tried to avoid it, to put it in the back of my head—out of sight, out of mind. But the mantra didn't work. Why should it? The incident had to be addressed and its meaning identified to prevent a reoccurrence. I wouldn't allow a moment like that to happen again, to be overwhelmed and become a burden to those around me. I knew what sparked the incident, just not why.

One day, it came together as I thought about the mission in my favorite neighborhood, about watching the bodies bounce around in those wheelbarrows. But it was strange. I still didn't feel bad for those men I killed. I feel no remorse for any of them. They were evil men, and I hated them. I still hate them. Not because my government told me to or because the media crafted an influential narrative. I hate what they stood for, what they did, and what they forced me and my friends to do. They were the personification of what's wrong in the world. I was proud to have played my part. But something inside me disagreed. So, I thought harder about the mission. I thought beyond the men and my anger. I thought about them as more than ISIS.

I stopped thinking about the fighter, the soldier. Whether ISIS, the Iraqi military, or even our coalition, I needed to see everyone differently. Instead, I thought about the people around them. As soon as I did that, I couldn't help but think about the people around me. I'm a soldier, resigned to my life choice; I accept the inherent danger of the job. This is true in any nation, although some militaries aren't filled with volunteers. But I'm more than that. I'm more than a weapon or a government tool of destruction. I'm a father, a husband, a brother, an uncle, and a son.

And so were they. The flood of emotions overtook me again as I had this realization.

I cried that day for the first time in years. I wept for my mother, whom I burdened by going off to war, my wife, whom I often abandoned for months on end, and my kids, who should never have had to imagine their father not coming home.

My heart also ached for the strangers I didn't know. The old woman in the Middle East who will never find her son's remains, mangled and buried in rubble. The young child, who waits for their father to come home, unaware he is in an unmarked grave somewhere in the desert. The pregnant lady, resolved to be strong even though she will raise that child alone, her husband at the bottom of the Euphrates River.

Something awoke in me that day, something long buried in my youth by a boy raised without a father, a boy trying to be a man too early. That day, I felt empathy, an invaluable trait I will instill in my sons.

It's easy for me to walk a mile in the shoes of a soldier, even an enemy soldier, because I am one. I understand the burdens of the young man risking his life, the thrill of doing something great, and the bonds of brotherhood gained through shared hardships. That day was different, though. It was somehow harder. Instead, I walked a mile in the shoes of a loved one, someone who didn't choose the military life but is a part of it regardless, suffering a very different burden than the soldier on the ground. That experience was eye-opening, and I haven't considered war in the same way since.

Seeing my family in that situation, I knew something needed to change in my life. I couldn't be the one in the wheelbarrow; I couldn't do that to my family. It quickly became apparent this was no longer my path. I needed something different, something new; I needed meaning and purpose again if I was going to stay in the Army. I decided to leave the tactical Army a few months after the incident at the pumpkin patch. I knew for a long time that I needed change, but I was scared to stop doing something I was good at, even if I wasn't happy doing it. So, I left the artillery branch in 2020.

My third kiddo was born a few years later and, as I have gotten older, my perspective has started to change. My time as a young man trying to prove himself has passed. Although I still serve and may even deploy again, my role is drifting further and further from the tactical fight. While I still wear the uniform, my job is fundamentally different. I became an Army strategist, hopeful that I could start influencing the military through my words and thoughts.

But that doesn't mean I can't still be "the rocket guy." I found a passion, even if I won't be the one firing them anymore. Instead of developing new tactics, techniques, and procedures, I've started to approach the topic from new angles, conducting broader and more applied research. I started to write. A lot. I challenged how rockets are reshaping conventional deterrence in Europe, highlighted the strategic implications of a missile treaty's demise, and rambled about integrating emerging technologies like loitering munitions and lethal autonomous weapons. Moving forward in my career, I know my part in the next war will be done with a pen.

My little dudes are quickly turning into young men. While I won't push the military life on them as a career, it wouldn't surprise me if they choose to chart a similar path as their old man. I dread the day I stop having empathy for the family members left behind and start being one myself. I know that, on that day, I will return to that field, my favorite neighborhood in Iraq, or maybe to how I imagine the wasteland of their generation. I will return there in my dreams as a father worried for his sons and the young soldiers he calls brothers, hands gripped tight on my wheelbarrow, ready to clean up the battlefield and embrace my role on the sidelines in the next generation's war. This is my burden.

But I don't know what type of conflict the next generation will face. I've seen firsthand how technological warfare makes it easier to kill. For the superior force, it makes war safer, and the danger is grossly asymmetrical. I don't know if this will lead to more morally ambiguous situations, instances where people remove themselves from the burden of war, killing without consequence, or allowing lethal autonomous weapons to do it for us. Warfare is evolving for those on the battlefield and in the air-conditioned offices of strike cells. This is something society will have to navigate through.

However, for the ones back home, the loss will be felt just as keenly. Through this lens, this empathy with the families on both sides of the conflict, I recalibrated my moral compass amid the ambiguity of modern war.

I've accepted that it's wrong to kill. At the same time, I believe it may be necessary. This duality was essential for me in reconciling how I felt about the war. I'm proud of the part I played in exterminating ISIS. At the same time, I'm glad a few moments are difficult to think about, a reminder I'm not a monster. I've also embraced the reality that it's healthy to find humor in difficult situations; otherwise, the world is depressing. So, I still look back and sometimes laugh at some of my missions, but it's more at bizarre circumstances than anything else. And that's okay because it's how I process the experience, and it's my journey to take. You were only along for the ride, glimpsing behind the curtain.

AFTERWORD

Writing About Warfare

> *Writing this was a rollercoaster of emotions; every soldier should tell their story.*

The world is saturated with tales from the Global War on Terror, with combat experiences in Iraq and Afghanistan the defining moments for many in my generation. These stories come from all walks of life, covering every perspective from the infantry soldier to the interpreter, from the general to the widow. People are comfortable with the narrative of the young lieutenant conducting patrols, the infantry squad building relationships with the local populace, and the general hardships of military deployments.

But this trip was unique. My role—the role of the US military as a whole—was not physically on the battlefield, yet we fought the war every day. And we suffered differently. It's a story that needed to be told. In turn, this reflection was a complex examination of the personal experiences that linger with me, the memories likely to resurface at random times in my life, and the guilt I carry with me for not only being proud of our successes but for continuing to revel in some of the unique tales.

This book offered a glimpse behind the curtain, away from the drama and narrative of the modern recounting of war. In doing so, some readers likely found this honesty disturbing. I'm sorry for that, but the truth is more important than the perception. The average citizen may be horrified to discover how easy it is for someone to laugh at brutality or for one to take pleasure in such a grave undertaking. I hope this account doesn't cast a shadow over the image of service members that society has put on a pedestal. At the same time, it's essential to highlight that the military is full of inherently fallible humans, simply a reflection of our society and not some elite warrior class.

The first reason for starting this journey and capturing my experience in Iraq was professional, to do my part as an aspiring military historian. Operation *Inherent Resolve* is a significant military campaign that merits further attention and analysis. I've been discouraged by the general lack of knowledge concerning this war when sharing my story. The later parts of our "forever war" in Iraq have disappeared from the spotlight, overshadowed by other significant world events.

But those who were there, the service members who took part in the liberation of major Iraqi cities, are responsible for not letting the conflict and its associated lessons be lost. My fear is this vital part of America's history in the Middle East will be lumped into broader conflicts in the region, treated merely as a continuation of the 2003 Iraq War. At the same time, capturing the essence of Operation *Inherent Resolve* includes more than just examining the 2014 recommittal of US forces into Iraq or the contested battle for Mosul—critical events that will undoubtedly dominate the historical retelling of this war.

Instead, military historians will discover we fought this conflict differently from previous operations in Iraq. In fact, the strike warfare conducted in Iraq between 2015 and 2017 may very well serve as a precursor to understanding the modern technological fights that followed. For example, the character of more recent conflicts, such as the 2020 Nagorno-Karabakh War between Armenia and Azerbaijan and the ongoing Russian incursion into Ukraine, are starkly different from the decades-long counterinsurgency fights the US military had experienced in Iraq and Afghanistan. An examination of Operation *Inherent Resolve* may serve as a bridge to understanding the growing reliance on lethal drones, the challenges of operating on a transparent battlefield, and the moral quagmire that comes from simplifying lethality. I hope my story can add to the knowledge base of this unique type of warfare, this technological fight, serving as a jumping-off point for future research projects.

The second reason is personal. I was surprised to find some memories from this trip to Iraq have stayed with me in a way I didn't initially appreciate, experiences that were fundamentally different from my previous deployments. These are memories I needed to share, even with the knowledge that challenging conversations surrounding them would likely follow. Nonetheless, they needed to be explored. These are not conversations I can sit down and have with those close to me. I fear their judgment. I'm not brave enough to see the disappointment in my mother's eyes when I smile at recounting a mission that ended gruesomely or face my wife's tears when I acknowledge my internal moral struggle with what I did to those men.

I also felt the need to leave an account for my children. In telling this story, I was determined to deglamorize the Hollywood image of warfare. Instead, I tried to offer them a dose of reality, an honest view of the soldier and how I thought about my duty. In doing so, I hoped to highlight the importance of empathy, even for the bad guys.

But I'm lucky. While I sometimes think about my experiences in Iraq and Africa, it's often fondly. In general, my deployments were great adventures that gave me unique stories to tell. In contrast, I have served with many soldiers who have faced horrors, lost loved ones, were forced to live in a constant state of hypervigilance, or regretted to their core an action they took, losing themselves to a war our society no longer cares about, if it ever did. Occasionally, I think about what could have happened if things had gone differently, about the burden I put on my family and the fear they faced in losing someone they love. In these moments, I think most about what I've done, about the families I destroyed and the young men we slaughtered.

In writing this, I could express feelings I couldn't recount any other way. Many service members, past and present, are struggling mentally and emotionally with their combat experiences. For some, it has taken them away from the service. For others, away from this world. For most, it's something minimal. A fleeting feeling on a bad day or a sad memory after a drink, even feeling guilty about finding humor in things you know you shouldn't or proud of an action that led to the death of other human beings. This doesn't mean they can no longer perform their duties or reintegrate into society. However, more often than not, expressing these thoughts is challenging and sometimes embarrassing, but I refuse to let these feelings fester, and neither should they. Writing this memoir and reflecting on warfare has been therapeutic for me, a more comfortable way to broach these uncomfortable topics. I hope that by sharing I can inspire others to do the same.

Acknowledgments

First and foremost, I want to thank my wife, Angela, who read several drafts and encouraged me throughout the writing process. Not only did you help me overcome my fear of sharing this personal account, but you helped make it readable by providing some hard truths along the way. I also want to thank my boys—Bradley, Benjamin, and Bryan. While they are not old enough to read this account, they remain my intended audience. Their support and encouragement motivate me every day.

I could not have done this project without the rest of my family. To my mom, Karon, my brothers Devin and Dylan, and my aunt Beth, thank you for reading my early manuscript. Your feedback was invaluable to improving the readability, and the challenging and emotional conversations that ensued are precisely why I needed to share my experience. Thank you for being a part of this journey.

A special thanks to the exceptional beta readers who played a critical role in this book's development: Bern Mulvey, Paul Milas, Ben Jackman, Michael Lynch, and Ben Underwood. Your candid feedback greatly enhanced the quality of this book.

Additionally, I would like to thank all the soldiers who sent me photos. While not all made the cut, those provided by Chris Rondel and Kara Dasalla were great additions to my story.

Finally, I would be remiss if I didn't thank the artillery men and women who made this possible. While this starts with the soldiers of the 1st Battalion, 94th Field Artillery Regiment, and the 17th Field Artillery Brigade, the burden of the indirect-fire service member extends well beyond this one deployment. I want to thank every Redleg, past and present, for what they do. There is a toll for launching artillery rounds down range, knowing full well the destruction it will cause. This burden is mitigated, at least to an extent, in the trust that the target and the cause are worthwhile. I think our cause was worth the burden, and I am thankful the Thunderbolt soldiers placed their trust in me.